THE DREW PARK SHARKS

VOICES FROM THE ALL-BLACK SWIM TEAM THAT PRODUCED ASTRONAUTS, JUDGES, AND CHAMPIONS

Gary Kimble

ISBN: 979-8-89079-494-9 (hardcover)
ISBN: 979-8-89079-495-6 (paperback)
ISBN: 978-1-64184-000-2 (ebook)

TABLE OF CONTENTS

Introduction v

Stanley McIntosh 1

Ellis R. Pearson 4

Benjamin Lindbergh Jeffcoat 8

James "Jimmie" Ruff 15

Chris Cochran 19

Charles Bolden, Jr. 23

Delano "Domino" Boulware 29

Tony Thomas 34

Gary E. Bell, Doctor of Health Administration (DHA) . . . 39

Stephen McIntosh 44

Moses Hopkins 48

Thaddeus Bell, MD 52

Dr. Harvey Dorrah, PhD 59

Regina Brandyburg Crump 63

Freddie Brandyburg 66

Talmadge Dixon 70

Robert "Pluto" Bradley 73

Howard "Porky" Simmons 77

Mark Harkness. 81

Richard "Kip" Harkness 85

Montez Martin, Jr. 88

Milton Kimpson 93

Edwina Fields. 97

Wesley Kennedy. 100

Carolyn Fair 104

Ronald Anderson 108

Dr. Virginia Brown Lockhart 113

Delores Brown 117

Karen Brown 119

Henry Kennedy 121

Spectators' Observations:
    David Whaley and James Edwards 126

Rupert A. Brown, Jr. 130

Yolande Kearse Lewis 133

Grant Lewis 136

LaVerda Kearse James. 139

Jusef "JD" Lewis. 149

Conclusion. 155

Appendix 157

INTRODUCTION

History has the potential to lift or devastate your spirit. Our history requires us to see both the good and the evil and to know right from wrong. As Dickens wrote in *A Tale of Two Cities*, "It was the best of times, it was the worst of times." History demonstrates that extreme contradictions can exist at the same time. Such is the story of the Drew Park Sharks of Columbia, South Carolina.

With Abraham Lincoln's Emancipation Proclamation signed on January 1, 1863, enslaved people in the Confederate states were declared free. The government, as stated in the document, would recognize all enslaved persons in the rebelling states. In addition, the proclamation allowed Black men to serve in the military, which strengthened the Union army. The Civil War ended on May 26, 1865, and with it, the dissolution of the Confederate States of America.

Following the Civil War, as early as later in 1865, and after the ratification of the 13th Amendment, Southern legislators passed state and local laws that enforced racial segregation throughout the late 19th century and early 20th century. The 13th Amendment formally abolished slavery and involuntary servitude, except as punishment for a crime. Many of these laws remained in effect until 1965. The laws were designed to disenfranchise and remove any political and economic gains made by African Americans during the Reconstruction era. Reconstruction was the period dominated by the challenges of the abolition of slavery. The laws were commonly referred to as Jim Crow Laws. Jim Crow laws mandated racial segregation in all public facilities in the former Confederate states. They detailed where and how formerly enslaved people could work and how much compensation they could receive. The laws basically put Black citizens into indentured servitude, and they took away voting rights and controlled where they lived and how they traveled. The U.S. Supreme Court in 1896 upheld Jim Crow laws and laid out its "separate but equal" legal doctrine concerning facilities for African Americans, in the case, Plessy v. Ferguson. Although in theory, the "equal" segregation doctrine governed public facilities and transportation, facilities for African American citizens were consistently inferior and underfunded compared to the facilities for white Americans. Sometimes there were no facilities for the Black community. Frequently, former Confederate soldiers worked as police officers and judges, making it difficult for African Americans to win court cases and ensuring they were subject to Black Codes.

In 1954, the segregation of public schools was declared unconstitutional in the landmark Supreme Court case, Brown v. Board of Education of Topeka. Any remaining Jim Crow laws were overturned by the Civil Rights Acts of 1964 and the Voting Rights Act of 1965.

In 1911, the City of Columbia Parks and Recreation Department opened the Maxcy Gregg Park. The park was named for a former Confederate general. In 1949, a swimming pool and bathhouse were dedicated. The pool was later renovated. It became a 50-meter pool, key for competitive swimming, as that is the official length for long-course events. At its previous length, swimmers' times did not translate to those at regulation pools, and top competitive events shunned the pool for that reason.

Drew Park opened in 1946 as a segregated recreational space for African Americans. It was originally called Seegers Park for the white family who had previously owned the land. To offer a more representative name, it was posthumously renamed in 1952 for Dr. Charles R. Drew, a prominent African American surgeon who was a pioneer in blood transfusions.

A 50-meter/55-yard swimming pool was opened in May 1950. The city compiled a group of highly skilled individuals to manage the complex. The swimming pool was a point of pride for Drew Park because of the neighborhood's highly successful men's and women's swimming teams, the Drew Park Sharks. The Sharks swim team was officially established in 1952. Beginning on Memorial Day and continuing through the summer, ending on Labor Day, the Drew Park pool was a lifesaving resource for the community, and many who swam there referred to it as their "summer babysitter." African American youth could go to the pool in the morning, stay through lunch, and have parents pick them up after work. As the number of competitive swim teams of color was limited and travel costs were prohibitive, the big event of the summer was generally the August intrateam swim meet. The meet drew a huge crowd of spectators and proud parents, relatives, and neighbors cheering on their favorite swimmers in each swimming event. In 2005, the Charles R. Drew Wellness Center opened, offering the community a modern 25-meter swimming pool, a gymnasium, a track, and a cardio workout center.

The writer recently found an AI-generated statement claiming, "There isn't much information about all-Black swim teams in South Carolina." The writer's goal is to change that statement.

Amidst all the negative issues surrounding the period of segregation, there was a committed group of individuals, really visionaries, who organized, managed, and coached African American youth to successful and impactful swimming experiences that altered their lives forever. It was due to the efforts of the numerous staff hired by the city over the decades, as well as other Black leaders, that the Drew Park Sharks became a reality. The staff members were known for their commitment to providing opportunities for Black youth in competitive swimming and for promoting swimming skills, fostering teamwork, and encouraging a love of the water in the community. The Sharks not only focused on developing athletes' swimming abilities but also emphasized the importance of education and community involvement. This remains an essential focus today, particularly in areas where access to swimming has been limited.

Throughout the stories related below, you will read about the events the Sharks competed in during their swim meets as well as the individuals themselves. At the Drew pool, different events were organized by age group.

The following were the swim events at Drew for the various age groups, as shared by Benjamin Lindbergh Jeffcoat:

Midget Boys and Midget Girls: Ages 0–10

> 50-meter freestyle; 50-meter breaststroke; 50-meter backstroke; 50-meter butterfly

Boys and Girls: Ages 11, 12, 13

> 50-meter freestyle; 50-meter breaststroke; 50-meter backstroke; 50-meter butterfly; 100-meter freestyle; 100-meter breaststroke; 100-meter backstroke; 100-meter butterfly

Junior Men and Women: Ages 14, 15, 16

> 50-meter freestyle; 50-meter breaststroke; 50-meter backstroke; 50-meter butterfly; 100-meter freestyle;

100-meter breaststroke; 100-meter backstroke; 100-meter butterfly; 200-meter freestyle; 200-meter breaststroke; 200-meter backstroke; 200-meter butterfly; 400-meter individual medley

Senior Men and Women: Ages 17 and higher

50-meter freestyle; 50-meter breaststroke; 50-meter backstroke; 50-meter butterfly; 100-meter freestyle; 100-meter breaststroke; 100-meter backstroke; 100-meter butterfly; 200-meter freestyle; 200-meter breaststroke; 200-meter backstroke; 200-meter butterfly; 400-meter individual medley; 800-meter freestyle (men only)

In the events at Drew, women and men swam separately. Most meets were all day on Saturdays. The Drew Park pool complex had, in addition to nine lanes, four diving boards. During meets, there were diving competitions for 1-meter and 3-meter springboards. On certain Sundays throughout the summer, the lifeguards, whether current, former, or inspiring, performed a water show that truly was a "show" for the community. The divers utilized all four boards and performed synchronized diving routines. To add extra excitement and entertainment value, some of the dives featured crisscross patterns, with divers jumping in front of and over each other as they dove into the water. During some water shows, a "ring of fire" event occurred in which individuals dove through a ring of fire, and on some weekends, the women performed synchronized routines in the water to music.

This writer was not a competitive swimmer, nor was he ever a member of a swim team. He swims for pleasure and the health benefits, which research emphasizes: swimming offers a comprehensive range of benefits for physical and mental health, making it an excellent choice for an active and healthy lifestyle. It is accepted by most that swimming:

- Strengthens the heart
- Improves blood circulation, reducing the risk of cardiovascular diseases
- Enhances strength and endurance by engaging multiple muscle groups
- Reduces impact on joints due to the buoyancy of water, making it suitable for people with arthritis
- Promotes flexibility and range of motion
- Excellent calorie-burning activity contributing to weight management
- The repetitive and calming motions of swimming can help reduce stress and anxiety
- Swimming releases endorphins, which have mood-boosting effects
- Regular swimming can improve sleep and reduce insomnia
- Relatively inexpensive exercise requiring minimal equipment
- Reduces belly fat by burning overall body fat through high-calorie expenditures
- Engages a person's core muscles, strengthening the stomach
- Increases blood circulation in the brain
- Increases shoulder strength, back muscles, and leg muscles
- A low-impact exercise, suitable for individuals of all fitness levels

Becoming a competitive swimmer is not the goal of most individuals. Swimming is just a good exercise for the reasons stated above. For most, gaining the benefits of swimming simply requires consistency. Frequency is a key, as in most forms of exercise. There are tools often provided at the pool. Kickboards or fins can help build leg strength. A pull buoy will help the individual focus on upper-body strength and improve one's endurance, stroke technique, arm and shoulder strength, while making swimming easier and more enjoyable. Practicing exhaling underwater and breathing every three to five strokes enhances rhythm. Maintaining a straight body will reduce drag, making swimming easier and improving the experience for the individual. Hand paddles assist with developing a proper stroke.

As a non-competitive swimmer, at times during this writing, various individuals categorized the Drew Park pool and the swimming events using different lengths. This made for some confusion. So as not to further confuse the reader, one needs to understand that the variations were purely personal preferences among the swimmers in describing the length of the events. Some individuals refer to the pool as 50 meters, while others refer to it as 55 yards. Specifically, some team members indicated they swam the 110, while others referred to it as the 100. The distances are virtually the same: 100 meters converts to 109.361 yards (110), and 50 meters converts to 54.6807 or 55 yards. Explaining the distance in another context, the 110-yard swimming event is comparable to swimming 10 yards more than the length of a football field.

Throughout this work, the reader will learn about the competitive races and which strokes the individual Sharks preferred. In swimming, there are four basic strokes: freestyle, backstroke, breaststroke, and butterfly. The freestyle, or front crawl as it is sometimes called, requires a streamlined body position and rotational momentum in the arms. The backstroke requires long strokes while laying of the back without seeing ahead. The breaststroke uses slow strokes and an understanding of how to avoid drag to increase total power. Finally, the butterfly is said to be the most difficult as it utilizes every muscle in the body to establish rhythm. These four strokes make swimming a more involved sport, unlike biking or running, where the athlete basically learns one technique. As with most swimmers, the individual Sharks needed to be proficient in more than one stroke, and in some cases, all four strokes. This is a testament to the work ethic and abilities of these young athletes. The reader will learn later how the techniques were required to be performed perfectly in competitions.

Not to minimize history in any way, but this is not a story about racism and the negativity surrounding the Drew Park Sharks. This is a story about the positive opportunity individuals experienced competitively swimming as members of the Drew Park Sharks. I would be remiss if I didn't highlight the extensive influence that the parents of these swimmers played in their success, both as swimmers and for their lives in general.

The following stories are conversations between the writer and former members of the Drew Park Sharks. The writer remembers the specific morning at the Drew Wellness Center in Columbia, South Carolina, casually chatting with Mr. Stanley McIntosh. Stanley turned to the writer and said, "Gary, I wish someone would write the history of the Sharks." The writer responded, "Well, Stanley, you are the history, and if you tell me your history, I will write it down." The writer met with Stanley shortly after in his office at the Drew Wellness Center. The writer carried an ink pen and a notepad. The writer listened to Stanley's personal history, taking notes as he shared his experiences. Due to the phenomenal relationships the Sharks developed and the admiration they shared, the Sharks forged deep friendships that have endured for generations. Each of them has maintained amazing connections with one another, to the point of cell phone numbers, knowledge of where each resides and their family lives, and the ability to reach out at a moment's notice. One cell phone call led to another and another, and in a short amount of time, the writer was on the way to a superb collection of conversations and personal histories, one could only imagine. The writer was honored to meet Ellis Pearson and hear his story of living in Saxon homes and his mother's loving support for him to join the swim team, while sitting in the lobby of an auto window tinting company. Lindy Jeffcoat invited the writer into his father's home; Tony Thomas, his karate studio; "Domino" Boulware, his office at Greenview Park; and the list went on and on. Fortunately, due to cell phones, the writer met several former Sharks via phone conversations from throughout South Carolina, and states including Alabama, California, Georgia, Maryland, Michigan, Virginia, Ohio, and the Federal District of Washington, D.C. Many invited the writer into their homes or places of business. The conversations shared were solely from the memories of the participating Sharks, and on occasion, two different former Sharks might have remembered an event slightly differently. The Sharks involved in these conversations were all born between 1934 and 1961, until the final conversation with JD Lewis, who was born in 1978.

This writer has written articles for his professional associations' newsletters and journals. He has given speeches at Black History Month celebrations and has served as president of the Mississippi Association of Housing Officers and the Southeastern Association of Housing Officers. He served one term as secretary of the Association of College and University Housing Officers – International during his thirty-seven years working in higher education. He was the 2008 recipient of the James Grimm Leadership and Service Award, a Founder's Award recipient, and was awarded the Charles W. Beene Memorial Service Award within his profession. Prior to that, he was employed in public schools in Ohio for five years. He has challenged his athletes prior to competitions while serving as the varsity cross-country coach at John Glenn High School in New Concord, Ohio. Looking back on that time, it was about all he knew about the space program and astronauts, until he had a conversation with Charles Bolden, Jr. That conversation is a part of this work. This is the first book for the writer, and he hopes the reader finds the conversations uplifting and inspirational, and a testament to what can be achieved with an opportunity.

The writer wishes to introduce these former competitive members of the Drew Park Sharks.

STANLEY MCINTOSH

Never have the words "life-altering" been more appropriate than when used to describe Stanley McIntosh's involvement with the Drew Park Sharks. Born in Germany in 1956 to a US military family, Stanley, following his mother's wish for him to learn to swim, signed up for swim lessons at Drew Park. Stanley's family had relocated to the Greenview area of Columbia, and at the age of nine, Stanley was learning to swim. By the age of ten, Stanley was a member of the Sharks swim team. Stanley's mom was a stay-at-home mom, and each day she drove him and his brother, Stephen, to the Drew pool, about ten minutes from their home.

For Stanley, being a Shark ignited a passion that has remained firmly intact for decades and guided his life's work. Being a Shark offered not only a life skill set but also relationships that have endured to this day. At fifteen, Stanley became a lifeguard at the Drew Park pool. Stanley stated his father gave him an allowance of ninety-nine cents each month, but as a lifeguard, he earned ninety-nine cents per hour. It was a staggering amount to him and made possible only through his involvement with Drew Park. It was just the first event in Stanley's life in which his association with Drew Park and the Drew Park Sharks impacted his life's decisions.

Stanley swam for the Sharks throughout high school, and that experience, once again, found benefit and meaning when he was awarded a small swimming scholarship to attend

South Carolina State University. During high school, Stanley swam the 100-meter breaststroke, and at South Carolina State University, he swam the 200-meter breaststroke. When Stanley arrived at South Carolina State University, he was in awe of the level of swimming skill and competitiveness his teammates displayed. Many had been involved in long-established swimming programs from several states, and Stanley could not believe such talented swimmers and programs existed. That knowledge and experience would once again impact his life, as he developed a commitment to pursuing quality swimming programs. When the South Carolina State University swim team had a swim meet, it was always scheduled on the same day as the men's basketball team game. In that way, the two teams could travel together on the same bus with the swim meet always in the afternoon prior to the evening basketball game. Stanley swam at South Carolina State for three of his four years in attendance. He thought he might enjoy football, but after just one year, he returned to the pool. He graduated in 1978 with a major in fine arts and a minor in education. After graduation, Stanley worked as a middle school teacher for two years. Following that, he became the assistant director of Greenview Park. He also served as pool manager during the summer months.

Stanley has coached the Greenview Dolphins for over forty years. He has served on the USA Swimming's Diversity, Equity, and Inclusion Committee for the past five years. While serving the committee, USA Swimming has flown him all over the country. Stanley has witnessed, firsthand, African American swim programs across this country, including aquatic centers and outdoor pools where minority children learn to swim and compete in facilities far larger than anything in Columbia, South Carolina. The Adamsville Aquatic Center in Atlanta, on Martin Luther King Jr. Drive, is a three-level community center with a 50-meter pool for minority children. The recreation department buses children from school to after-school activities at the community center, offering programs such as tutoring, basketball, swim lessons, a swim team, and much more.

Since becoming a Drew Park Shark at the age of ten, Stanley's passion has only grown during his lifetime. He has committed his life to the development of youth, many of whom have gone on to achieve success in a variety of endeavors. Today, Stanley continues to serve as coach of the Greenview Dolphins Swim Team, though the title of coach does not encompass all that Stanley is able to achieve as a city influencer and promoter of minority programs throughout Columbia, the State of South Carolina, and beyond.

ELLIS R. PEARSON

From the outset of your conversation with Ellis Pearson about Drew Park, it is obvious that there is a love and respect for the park and facilities that gave his life direction and a sense of achievement and satisfaction. His voice is honestly unable to hold back his appreciation for what Drew Park gave him, both in the form of opportunity and in keeping his life straight and decent, and out of trouble.

Ellis was born in 1955 and raised in Columbia, though he also lived in other places because his father was a military man. Ellis' mother cleaned houses and worked in her sister's family restaurant. They lived in Saxon Homes, barely 100 yards away from the Drew Park swimming pool. The area was later demolished to make way for the current Drew Wellness Center. Ellis recalls how massive Drew Park was, with an outdoor basketball court, baseball field, tennis courts, an indoor recreation center, a huge parking lot, and concrete stadium seating overlooking a 55-yard (50-meter) pool with four diving boards. To Ellis, it was like a country club. African Americans from counties and towns near and far often visited Drew Park because of its facilities, particularly the pool. Few facilities of such quality were available to African Americans, and summer holidays frequently saw massive crowds.

Ellis was a self-taught swimmer. He was eleven years old when he began swimming. He mowed lawns for the Saxon residents to earn money to pay pool fees. He swam every day of the summer, and at night, he often had difficulty sleeping because of his excitement for the next day at the pool. On his first dive from the pool's diving board, Ellis had to be rescued by the lifeguard. After that, he was determined to learn to swim so he could use the diving board. At twelve, Ellis joined the team and became an official Shark. He reported that on the first day of practice, the coach worked Ellis and his friends really hard, and after that, several of Ellis' friends sneaked away and did not return. Ellis was too afraid to follow his friends, so he remained at practice. After practice that evening, Ellis told his mother he no longer wanted to swim. The next day, his mother took him to swim team practice.

In his first competitive meet, Ellis did not do well. The next summer, Ellis started putting in extra time at practice, swimming laps with Jimmie Ruff. Jimmie was a good distance swimmer, but Ellis, now sixteen, had worked hard and was confident. He felt he could not only beat Jimmie but also everyone else on the team. At one meet, Jimmie didn't compete. Ellis had a little competition from some of his teammates, but he was determined, and he had worked hard to become a better distance swimmer. Ellis won both the 880-yard and the 440-yard events that summer. Ellis also swam both the individual medley and the medley relay. Ellis stated his backstroke was his weakest stroke, but he made up for that shortcoming with a very strong breaststroke, butterfly, and freestyle. Ellis worked as a lifeguard in addition to competing in swimming. At the Drew pool, lifeguards also gave swimming lessons as part of their job responsibilities. Ellis stated he gave his mother part of his weekly pay to assist with the family's expenses.

In 1971, Ellis met Pete Combs. Pete was the white coach at the University of South Carolina, and he was coaching an AAU team at Trenholm Park, a 25-yard indoor pool. In an 800-yard race, Ellis beat Pete, who was in his late twenties or early thirties. Following that race, Pete invited Ellis and another swimmer,

Benjamin Jeffcoat, to join the team at Trenholm Park. In 1970, the pool had integrated, but Pete needed a month to convince parents to allow Ellis and Benjamin to swim on the team. During that month, Ellis and Ben swam early in the mornings, alone before school. Once the parent group granted approval, they became the first two African Americans to swim with the team. He felt very comfortable and accepted by the team. They traveled with the team to a meet in Aiken as the only two Black kids on both teams. The relay team did well, as Ellis recalled.

Ellis wasn't bothered by being a Black member of the all-white team. It didn't really faze him. Being a military kid, he had started first grade at an integrated school in Washington State, where his father was stationed. Entering restaurants through the back door, sitting in the back of the bus, and watching movies from the theater's balcony were just things that happened. Ellis never allowed the racial situations to bother him.

In addition to swimming, during his senior year in high school, Ellis joined the track team, where he ran the one-mile and two-mile races. He was as successful in running distance races as he was in swimming distance races. Running remained part of Ellis' life, and he competed throughout the years after high school. Following high school, Ellis decided to join the Marine Corps. Although he had been offered a four-year scholarship to swim at South Carolina State University, he had his heart set on the Marines. One day, while at Camp Lejeune, a captain saw Ellis swimming and encouraged him to join the Fleet Swim Team. The captain was also a swimmer, and whether the captain swam in the competition determined whether Ellis placed first or second. Ellis was stationed in Italy for a couple of years and raced in several running competitions, generally doing very well. In 1975, Ellis was stationed in Quantico, Virginia. The base had a very nice pool and was used by a white AAU team for practice. Ellis worked out with the team and assisted their female coach. After seven years, Ellis left the military and returned to Columbia. He returned to the Drew Park pool, competing in their swimming events. Drew Park encouraged swimming and, to maintain that interest, offered a variety of categories to accommodate the maximum number of competitors. Levels began as young as six years old, and there was even a category for men and women eighteen years and older. Once again, Ellis was offered a scholarship to swim at South Carolina State University, but after a year, wanting to earn more money, Ellis left the university. Ellis is currently employed by the Richland County Sheriff's Department.

BENJAMIN LINDBERGH JEFFCOAT

Whether you know him as Ben or Lindy, the one thing you know for certain is that in everything he has done, this man has always displayed a strong work ethic, commitment, determination, and the motivation to win. Lindy firmly believed that "swimming just depends on me being first." He attempted to play football and basketball, but quickly realized he didn't need to depend on a team. He only needed to "touch the wall" first and in the fastest time to earn the respect and support of those around him. It was his mindset that he didn't need other people, because at the pool, you were accepted by everyone if you captured first place. This is in no way to say that Lindy was not interested in his teammates. To the contrary, he was respected as an admired and appreciated member of the Drew Park Sharks, and he personally valued the camaraderie of the other swimmers. Being an only child, Lindy felt that his teammates were more like his brothers and sisters. He always said that at the end of the day, his fellow Sharks went home to their families, while he always went home to his parents. Lindy was well aware of what his success meant to the team's overall success. Whether in high school as a member of the Sharks or as a member of the South Carolina State University swim team, Lindy swam the race that was needed for the team's success. Lindy even swam medley events where he was required to swim the backstroke. It was a stroke he called "controlled drowning" and one that caused his teammates to jokingly run down the side of the pool carrying a ring buoy, ready to throw it to him at any point. Fortunately, Lindy was a strong, fast swimmer, and his other strokes in the medley race were more than sufficient for him to be successful even with his backstroke. The South Carolina State University mascot was the Bulldog, and the swim team called themselves the Aquadogs.

Born in 1956, Lindy and his family lived on Farrow Terrace in Columbia, South Carolina. In 1966, the family moved to Grand Street, where Lindy was raised. Lindy's father was an assistant principal at W.A. Perry Middle School, and his mother was a social worker for the Columbia Housing Authority. Each day during the summer, one of Lindy's parents dropped him off at Drew pool and the other brought him lunch. As others have stated, Lindy, too, said Drew was his "summer babysitter." Lindy said he was told he was about two years old when he first got "thrown into the water." As a Shark, he swam Midget Boys at age nine or ten. He set the record for the Midget Boys 50-meter freestyle at twenty-seven seconds, a record that still stands today. He swam in every age bracket at Drew Park, including Midget Boys ages 0–10; Boys ages 11, 12, 13; Junior Men ages 14, 15, 16; and Senior Men ages 17 and higher. Because Lindy's birthday was in September, he was often the youngest in his classes. He graduated at seventeen and entered South Carolina State University on a four-year swimming scholarship. He turned eighteen that September. Lindy's dad was always involved with him in his endeavors. Lindy recalls asking his dad once if he took him to the pool each day, and always offered to have his friends visit at home to keep an eye on him and know where he was at all times. His father responded, "Yes." Lindy's dad assisted in managing the team a couple of summers with the other full-time staff members at Drew pool. Lindy referred to his dad as a "hands-off/hands-on" dad.

There's a perception that the Drew Park Pool Sharks rarely competed against other teams. There was a large intra-squad competition at the end of each summer, which drew huge crowds from the community. Each swimming event had as many as nine participants. But, in reality, the Sharks swam against several other all-Black swim teams from towns such as Charleston, Greenwood, Greenville, Aiken, and Orangeburg. Each year, teams rotated hosting, and, unfortunately, in some years, some teams did not participate. In those years, it appeared that the intra-squad competition was the major event of the summer. For swim meets not hosted at Drew, the swimmers traveled in their parents' cars to the meets.

Speaking of competitions, Lindy shared that there were race mechanics and regulations that had to be followed to avoid disqualification. Judges were assigned to monitor the swimmers' race mechanics to ensure proper race procedures and stroke techniques were being followed accurately and that the race was conducted fairly by all athletes. For example, today, there is a mandatory 15-meter underwater limit for the backstroke, butterfly, and freestyle strokes. During the time of the Sharks, that underwater limit was much shorter. There are specific two-hand touches where the hands are required to come together for the breaststroke and the butterfly stroke. For the freestyle stroke and the breaststroke, the judge will monitor the competitor keeping the body on the breast during the competition. Other mandates include remaining on your back unless you're executing a turn for the backstroke. In the breaststroke, the swimmer must perform a specific cycle of one-arm pull and one-leg kick simultaneously, with the head breaking the water surface at each cycle. Similar rules exist for the butterfly stroke. Clearly, competitive swimming requires practice and attention to detail to avoid disqualification during a race. The Drew Park Sharks were competent swimmers, and competitions were judged professionally. The reader can clearly see that the skills exhibited by the Sharks were nothing short of amazing for these young men and women.

After being noticed by Pete Combs, the swim coach of the all-white Trenholm Park team, Lindy was joined by Ellis Pearson to be a part of the team. The Trenholm pool was a short-course pool because it was 25 yards. Lindy recounted a story similar to Ellis's: They had to practice alone each morning before going to school because they needed permission from the white parents to swim at Trenholm, even though the pool had, in theory, integrated the prior year. Lindy believed it was a considerably longer period to get that approval than what Ellis recalled. Lindy said they practiced alone for nearly three months. While swimming for the Sharks, Lindy focused a great deal on speed, but under the guidance of Pete Combs at Trenholm, Lindy's attention and focus were more on technique and stroke alteration, or as Lindy stated, "finding new water." Lindy and Ellis swam year-round, which helped them become better swimmers. At the Trenholm pool, in the winter months, they swam yards, and during the summer at the Drew pool, they swam meters. Swim practice was two hours in the afternoon with swims of 4,000 to 5,000 yards Monday through Friday. At Trenholm (Richland County Swimming Association), Lindy swam the 50-yard freestyle, the 50-yard breaststroke, the 100-yard freestyle, and the 100-yard breaststroke. Acceptance at Trenholm Park was made much easier when Ellis and Lindy began winning competitively, and again, Lindy's belief that "touching the wall first" made all the difference. The team at Trenholm Park swam against several other teams from around the state, but no other team had integrated, leaving Lindy and Ellis the only African American swimmers in the competitions.

Like Stanley, Ellis, and many other members of the Drew Park Sharks, Lindy was a certified lifeguard and a certified Water Safety Instructor. In addition to being a lifeguard, they were qualified to teach swimming lessons. Returning lifeguards always received priority in positions for the next summer. When Lindy was old enough to be certified, there were no positions available at the Drew pool. He learned about a position at a Girl Scout campground and one in a subdivision called Crane Forest, which gave him summer employment. Once Lindy obtained a lifeguard position at Drew, he worked every summer and even returned each summer during college to work as a lifeguard. Generally, the pool had six lifeguards for the summer. The morning shift usually gave swim lessons, and the afternoon lifeguards generally assisted with the swim team. The swim team usually had one workout each day, practicing from around 6:00 p.m. to 8:00 p.m. The pool hours were 9:00 a.m. to 9:00 p.m. It had nine lanes, with five set aside for the team to practice. As a lifeguard, Lindy earned a modest income of around $1,000 to $1,500 per year.

Unlike many of the other swimmers on the team, Lindy was a student school bus driver for Columbia High School during his junior and senior years of high school. He had an elementary school and a middle school route each day, and on occasions, he drove a high school route. Lindy recalled that you could obtain a permit to drive at age fourteen, then you were required to wait thirty days before obtaining your driver's license. You could get your bus driver's license at age fifteen. This position paid him $1,000 per year. This provided him with additional income beyond what his parents provided, and, as a youth, he was able to open a bank account, which taught him financial responsibility. This contributed to his preparation for his adult life.

Although a sprinter throughout high school as a member of the Sharks, as a college freshman, the team already had a sprinter. Lindy moved from sprinting to the distance races, which he gladly accepted based upon the inspiration he had received from watching Jimmie Ruff, and for the good of the team. The coach, Robert Bradley (a former Shark), at South Carolina State University preferred that swimmers place first in events, rather than first and second. Thus, Lindy swam the multiple distance races. Being a freshman, he swam the 200, 500, and 1000-yard freestyle events. He remained a middle- and distance-swimmer throughout his college career as other sprinters continued to enter South Carolina State University. The longer swimming events required an experienced swimmer, causing Lindy to fill that role for the good of the team. He also swam anchor in the 4x100 freestyle relay team and anchor on the 4x100 medley relay team. In college, Lindy had two workouts each day, swimming 2,000 to 3,000 yards between 6:00 a.m. and 7:00 a.m., as well as swimming 4,000 to 5,000 yards between 4:00 p.m. to 6:00 p.m.

Swim season generally runs from November to March. It was typical for the team to travel on Thursday and swim Friday and Saturday. In addition to traveling with the basketball team, the wrestling team occasionally traveled with them on the team bus. South Carolina State University had a large stretch limo that the swim team used from time to time. The swim team competed head-to-head against many colleges and universities throughout the season. Some of the schools with swim teams included Howard University, Morgan State University, Delaware State University, Maryland Eastern Shore University, Texas Southern University, Albany State University, Furman College, The Citadel, the College of Charleston, and Morehouse College.

Each year on Thanksgiving Weekend, there was a large relay meet featuring four HBCU relay teams for every stroke, as well as a competitive 4x100 individual medley relay team event. Generally, the four HBCU teams came from a list that included Albany State University, Morehouse College, Texas Southern University, Howard University, Alabama A&M University, Hampton University, and Johnson C.

Smith University. Lindy was selected as the Most Promising Freshman swimmer at South Carolina State University and selected as the Most Valuable Player in his sophomore, junior, and senior years in college. He graduated from South Carolina State University with a degree in business administration. He worked for the State Farm Mutual Automobile Insurance Company as an adjuster, claims supervisor, and ultimately, he became a claims superintendent, always moving up within the system after being promoted several times to more responsible positions. In addition to his employment at State Farm, Lindy sold cars, where he assisted customers with financial counseling, enabling them to purchase cars, secure financing, and build their credit.

After taking some time off from collegiate swimming, Lindy took up both open water swimming and the occasional triathlon. He swam on the Master's level in open water. The distances varied, including 2.5 miles, 3 miles, and even a 5-mile course. He swam several swims in the Caribbean, as well as Siesta Key, Florida, and Charleston, South Carolina. In 2016, he swam his final event in St. Croix. You could probably categorize his triathlon competitions as short-lived. Lindy said it was not unusual for him to finish in 100th place among 100 athletes. He stated he struggled with the runs. To Lindy, running was like a punishment. He was late to practice once and was required to run laps, so he never liked the running component of a triathlon. For pleasure now, Lindy has become a certified scuba diver and has completed up to sixty dives as of this writing. He has remained faithful to the water. Lindy is currently retired and resides in Haines City, Florida.

JAMES "JIMMIE" RUFF

1940 – 2024

AS SHARED BY HIS WIFE, DORIS RUFF

In nature, the shark is described as bold, resilient, aggressive, powerful, ferocious, beautiful, intelligent, and majestic, and it displays social interactions. Its most acute sense is used to detect prey from a distance, and its electroreceptors or special sensory organs can detect the weak. To his competitors, Jimmie Ruff, probably often seemed to be more shark than Drew Park Shark. One of the earliest members of the swim team, Jimmie Ruff, was also one of the most revered, diligent, goal-oriented, and successful swimmers the team ever had. It was not unusual for one of the pool's staff members to ask if he was ever going to get out of the water to even eat. Doris noted that Jimmie swam with the smoothest strokes, displacing minimal water with each movement, gliding through the water. She said he was simply mesmerizing!

Born in Columbia in 1940, Jimmie Ruff (pronounced roof) grew up just blocks from the Drew Park pool in the Waverly community on Heidt Street, just past Benedict College. Jimmie's father was a pharmacist and owned a pharmacy. His mother was an elementary teacher. Jimmie began swimming around the age of ten. With the pool opening in May 1950, Jimmie became one of the earliest and youngest boys to swim at Drew Park. Jimmie's mother walked him the several blocks to the pool each day. Jimmie had a friend and fellow swimmer at the pool named Gus. Jimmie became a Shark while still in elementary school. He credited Gus, an older swimmer and mentor of sorts, for encouraging him to "go out and beat everyone." It was advice that Jimmie took to heart.

Speaking of heart, Jimmie's was full of encouragement to his fellow teammates. He was always supporting, encouraging, and challenging his fellow Sharks in the most positive manner, and his positive nature made folks do what he asked of them. Jimmie was that rare individual who was awesomely skilled and successful, while never losing sight of his responsibility to his fellow Sharks, as a good team member should be. Though he held several records across the various age categories of swimming at Drew, he never missed the opportunity to offer encouragement in his quiet, respectful manner. Jimmie's successes as a Drew Park Shark were widely known, and to this day, Doris has the "hardware," in the form of trophies, ribbons, and photographs she proudly shares and displays on his behalf.

It is thought that Jimmie became a lifeguard at fifteen, the minimum age at the time in 1954, and only five years after starting his swimming experience. Prior to that, he worked in the "basket" room. Jimmie was a distance swimmer by nature. You've already read how peers such as Ellis Pearson learned from Jimmie to become successful distance swimmers themselves. I have heard former Sharks say that Jimmie was one of the fastest swimmers they have ever seen. Though most were born long after him, many were able to witness him compete. Jimmie swam in just about every age division and just about every swimming event, if not all of them. He was a tremendous freestyle swimmer, and it was normal for him to finish in first place in the 220, 440, and 880-yard races. Jimmie was also an outstanding backstroke and breaststroke swimmer. The same could also be said about all four strokes in the 100-meter events. Lindy stated during our conversation that everyone looked up to Jimmie, not only for his speed and success in swimming but also for the support, kindness, generosity, and the leadership he provided to his fellow Sharks.

Jimmie developed a hobby in photography while in high school and had a dark room in his house. He loved taking photos, and today, many of the photos seen displayed at the Drew Wellness Center and other locations were taken and developed by Jimmie. Jimmie graduated from C.A. Johnson High School in 1957 and attended Benedict College, where he graduated with a degree in biology education in 1961. Jimmie was not permitted to become a Certified Water Safety Instructor in South Carolina, as it was illegal for Blacks to be certified in the State. Jimmie went to North Carolina, where he was certified. He taught middle school science at Lakeview High School. He went on to teach at Busby Middle School, where he also served as assistant principal, and later served as assistant principal at Northside Middle School and subsequently, Fulmer Middle School until 1996, when he retired.

An interesting note about Jimmie was that he taught swimming and diving classes at Drew pool for both Allen University and Benedict College students before each institution had a campus pool. By this period, Jimmie had gotten married to Doris, and she was an adult student in one of Jimmie's swim classes. The writer does not recall her sharing the grade she received in that particular college class.

After high school, Doris became a secretary at the elementary school where Jimmie's mom worked and where she was formally introduced to him. Following four years of dating, they were married in 1971. The couple has two children, James Jr. and April. James was born in 1978, and April was born in 1980. They both swam for the Sharks, but both had been swimming since birth. Ellis Pearson shared that he was actually April's swim teacher, as Jimmie felt she would probably listen and follow his directions better than if he had tried to teach her to swim. Doris relates how she enrolled in the "Mommie and Me" program with April when she was about two months old, and that one day, with JR (four months) in his arms, Jimmie jumped off the high dive with him. I don't believe a hive of angry hornets was a match for the emotions displayed by Doris when she learned of what Jimmie had done. Both JR and April became lifeguards at Drew pool. April went on to attend Francis Marion University, where she managed the campus pool. JR attended Coastal Carolina University for a time and worked as the assistant manager of the Greenview Park Pool.

Jimmie's relationship with the Drew pool was long and memorable. He served as the assistant coach and pool manager, and as a member of the City of Columbia search committee charged with developing plans for the Drew Wellness Center. Jimmie truly dedicated his life to swimming and guiding youth to successful lives. Jimmie always said he believed the pool represented hope and was a safe haven for young people. He was truly loved by all, and in turn, he had a deep connection with peers such as Stanley McIntosh. Jimmie often stated that Stanley was the man who "kept the dream alive" and that Stanley got the message to "stick with it." It was clear that Jimmie was one who passed on what he had learned to others for the benefit of future generations. Jimmie and Doris had a pool at their home, which Jimmie used until his Parkinson's Disease prevented him from coordinating his leg movements. He passed away in 2024.

CHRIS COCHRAN

Throughout my conversation with Chris Cochran, the word genuine was etched in my mind. As Chris spoke and shared his experiences as a Drew Park Shark, there was never any doubt that he was being honest, sincere, and authentic. I could sense the emotions he has carried with him his entire adult life regarding the opportunities that the Drew Park pool afforded him.

Although others have shared their feelings about the magnitude and opulence of Drew Park, with its vast array of athletic facilities, topped off by the outstanding pool, Chris' memories of the sprinkler pool, as well as the pool design and specifics, left no doubt that he was in awe of Drew Park. His detail as to the location of the ropes, which were used to delineate pool depths, clearly made an indelible mark on his memory, and it was real, as though they were still in existence today.

His appreciation, his admiration, his respect, and his desire to be like the older swimmers he watched burned like a flame in him that could not be extinguished. It was clear that Chris Cochran would work as hard as necessary to not let down those individuals who meant so much to him and whom he so greatly admired. He was determined to be their equal, and for them to be proud that he, too, was deserving of being a Shark. This is why Chris mastered the butterfly. For most swimmers, the butterfly was "like punishment," and most struggled to do it properly. To Chris, it was a stroke of beauty when done well.

It was a stroke that others admired because it not only required stamina and strong swimming skills, but it also just "looked good." It was a stroke Chris practiced, though it wasn't even his favorite stroke. Given the opportunity, Chris would swim the 50-meter freestyle anytime.

Born in Columbia in 1960, Chris grew up in Highland Park. Both of his parents were teachers and taught in several different schools. Chris's father was also a football coach. Chris played football throughout high school and swam in the summer. He began swimming around age ten or eleven. Going to the pool each day required transportation, and since his parents' friends were the Harkness family, Chris rode with them to Drew Park most days. Chris's memories of playing in the sprinkler pool with its 25-foot diameter, 4-inch rise, and the tall pole in the middle with the sprinklers were vivid. His description of the Drew Park pool itself helps everyone appreciate it more when one considers that the pool at Trenholm Park could fit width-wise inside the Drew pool. From side to side, the Drew Park pool was approximately 25 yards/meters. Length wise, it was 50 meters/55 yards. He took swim lessons from Stanley McIntosh, learning to swim the pool width wise at pretty much the same depth. The pool had three roped areas signaling its depth. The first section was 3–4 feet, the second 4–6 feet deep, and the third section 6–12 feet deep. The third section was for the pool's diving area.

Chris became a Shark in sixth grade. Around age thirteen, he was swimming in intermediate boys. Chris said his first coach made him swim everything at practice to strengthen his stroke skills, and that he also focused on speed and endurance. Chris attributed and paid homage to his coaches for pushing him and helping him become the swimmer he was. Chris became a lifeguard and was Water Safety Certified. This is a program sponsored by the Red Cross. Not all Drew Park Sharks were lifeguards, nor were all lifeguards Water Safety Certified.

Early on in his swimming, Chris tried to model himself after the older swimmers in order to swim in the deep water. He shared that some of the lifeguards were amazing divers, and that "he wanted to be like them." He said the lifeguards, like Stanley, offered both challenge and encouragement. At times, the guards engaged in "playful hazing."

Chris loved the water, and he practiced diligently all summer. Throughout our conversation, he frequently shared his appreciation for his coaches who pushed him hard. His first event to swim was the 200x4, and he was victorious. Chris says he is reminded to this day when he meets one of his former coaches, as if he would ever forget. The staff members who managed the pool were instrumental in ensuring it was properly maintained and received the recognition it deserved. It was a priority for them. Mediocrity was never acceptable. Like some of the other members of the Sharks, Chris drove a school bus during high school. As a junior, he drove a middle school and high school route, but during his senior year, he drove a handicapped student bus, which paid even more. As much as Chris enjoyed swimming, he enjoyed playing football. After high school, Chris attended Johnson C. Smith University in North Carolina. He had the opportunity to attend South Carolina State University, but the swim coach was adamant that he could not swim and play football. Chris chose Johnson C. Smith. He swam there for three years on a partial scholarship. He majored in urban studies/community development.

The swim coach at Johnson C. Smith University annually sponsored the J.C Smith Invitational. It was a team relay event. His coach thought it was a creative way to promote the sport of swimming. Several small schools participated, such as the University of North Carolina – Greensboro, Albany State University, Morehouse College, Miles College, and South Carolina State University. Like most meets, there were heats and semi-finals, and the final three top swimmers in each event were recognized as members of the "Black Collegiate All Americans," a name designated from the event. Chris was recognized for winning the 200-meter butterfly.

After college, Chris was hired by the Columbia Housing Authority. Lindy Jeffcoat's mother was his supervisor. Chris also spent five or six years with the Navy Reserves, and he has worked for the past twenty-plus years with the Lutheran Family Services, where he is currently employed. Chris uses many of the skills he learned as a lifeguard and as a school bus driver. He teaches defensive driving and CPR classes for the Lutheran Family Services. He also specializes in quality management and training new employees and team members. He continues to see himself as a "lifeguard," for if a new team member needs help, he jumps into action as if he were in the lifeguard chair. "You jump in the water to get them out, not asking questions until after they are safe."

During the Navy Reserves boot camp, the recruits were asked if anyone could swim. Chris volunteered that he had been a member of the Drew Park Sharks and a WSC lifeguard. He was asked to "rescue" one of the members of the reserves who thought he might make it difficult and prove that Chris was not the swimmer he had indicated. The pretending drowning victim rolled like an alligator and behaved in a panicking manner, which is exactly what Chris had been taught to anticipate when rescuing someone. Chris maintained his composure, dug his nails into the armpit of the "drowning victim" to quell his behavior, and delivered him to the surface. Everyone was in awe of Chris for having accomplished what Chris knew he was trained to do. The general comments from the other reservists were, "We've never seen a Black guy swim like that."

CHARLES BOLDEN, JR.

This writer was sitting at his laptop earlier today when he received a phone call. His first thought was he might require the services of one of the Drew Park Shark lifeguards with the certification to perform CPR, as on the other end of the cell phone was Charles Bolden, Jr. If one can imagine answering the phone to hear it is a world-famous United States astronaut, then you know how this writer felt.

It's not a stretch to think that there would have been no Drew Park or Drew Park pool as we know it without the dedicated staff members hired to manage it. It was a place of refuge for the hundreds of thousands of African Americans from around the city, area, and the state of South Carolina. A great debt is owed to the men hired over the decades. Charles Bolden Jr.'s mother was Ethel Martin Bolden, and his father was Charles Bolden, Sr. The reader will hear those names more throughout this work. Charles' father, Charles, Sr., served as one of the pool's staff members, and with others, they hired early lifeguards like John Brown and Jimmie Ruff and developed policies and procedures that created the successful pool environment.

Born in 1946, Charlie grew up three blocks from Drew Park. The family had constructed a new home in 1949, just one year before the Drew pool opened. Early in the pool's history, everyone was taught to swim by the staff, who wanted every African American kid to know how to swim. As the reader is aware, they wanted lifeguards to be certified, and many were WSI certified. Charles' father, Charles, Sr., was the assistant manager of Drew Park pool, and it's safe to say that he loved kids. In addition, his father coached high school football, track, basketball, and tennis. He taught history and civics after graduating from Johnson C. Smith. Charles' mom, Ethel Martin Bolden, also attended Johnson C. Smith and majored in English. She was a librarian and received her master's degree from Atlanta University.

Charles, Jr. shared he was much like a fish. He loved the water. After all, he began swimming at the age of four. Like many young men at Drew pool, Charles started working in the basket room and collecting entry tickets. If an individual brought any valuable item, it was placed in a safe at the pool. The complex had a large locker room, and swimmers would place their clothes, etc., in a basket and attach a tag or pin to identify it, which would be used when they left to retrieve their possessions. Charles indicated he believed the locker room area was as large as the one at Maxcy Gregg pool, but probably not as "equal" in amenities, with that "separate but equal" policy.

His favorite stroke to swim in competition was the butterfly, followed closely by the backstroke. He was also always a competitor in the medley relay, which the reader knows is the four-man competition in the backstroke, breaststroke, butterfly, and freestyle. Charles became a certified lifeguard and certified in WSI. He was a "first-generation Shark," being an early member of the team. He swam competitively from elementary school through high school, and he played on the football team. Charles disclosed that when he was young, he served as the water boy for the high school football team, which included Moses "Hop" Hopkins. Charles' father was the coach of the football team and of several other sports. Charles vividly recalls traveling to compete in swim meets. Jacksonville was always a great trip for the team. They swam at Edward Waters

University, an HBCU institution. The team also traveled to Greenville, Johnson C. Smith University, Augusta, and even to Tennessee to compete. At the time, the white newspapers covered all the swim teams, including the Black teams. It was easy to compare event times, specifically how you might compare with others who swam the same event, like on the white teams. Charles noted that South Carolina State University was clearly number one for swimming in South Carolina.

After graduating from high school, Charles received an appointment to the United States Naval Academy in Annapolis, Maryland. At the time, Charles indicated that one could select the service one wished to join upon graduation. Charles chose the Marines. Today, the system is different. It is a "service assignment." When you are a senior, you learn which service you will be joining. Charles had a close relationship with one officer named John Riley Love. He shared many of Charlie's father's personal characteristics and became a mentor to Charlie. He said of John Love, "His leadership captured me" because of his style and demeanor, and "I wanted to be like him." At the academy, he made several friends who had a profound impact on him. In addition to his feelings toward John Riley Love, he was impressed with Luke Thames. As a Marine, Charles anticipated he would be assigned to the infantry division, typically the ground troops that engage in close-range combat. It was generally considered that an infantry soldier's life expectancy was measured in weeks and months. Due to his high standing at the academy, Charles selected the "aviation option." He believed flight school would be a good insurance policy, though he had no desire to fly. In addition, his wife hated the idea of him being in the infantry. Charles went to Pensacola for aviation in "advanced jet" training. Following his first flight with Pete Fields, he fell in love with flying and knew he wanted to be a test pilot. He had no desire to be a "Blue Angel" for fear of the planes flying so near each other.

He earned his "wings" with the fleet of the A-6 Intruders and flew for seven years.

In 1978, Charles was accepted into test pilot school, and the following year, he graduated as a test pilot. He learned that NASA was looking to expand the shuttle program with civilian and military men and women, regardless of race. In 1978, thirty-five individuals were selected, including Sally Ride, Ron McNair, and Fred Gregory. Charles and Guion (Guy) Bluford were selected in the second group of fighter pilots for potential astronauts. Guy became the first African American to go into space. He participated in four space shuttle flights between 1983 and 1992. Before being accepted into the class of astronauts, Charles spoke with Ron McNair. Ron McNair happened to be attending a reunion near Charles' home. Charles met him when he was getting off the plane. Charles said he ran to introduce himself to Ron as he was getting off his plane. Charles took him home with him to meet his family, and they spent the weekend talking about the space program. Their conversation went something like this:

> Ron: "Are you going to apply to the space program?"
> Charles: "They'd never pick me."
> Ron: "That's the dumbest thing I ever heard."

That evening, Charles informed his wife he was applying for the space program. Charles reports that his father had just passed away, so he was never given the opportunity to share the decision with his dad. Thus, Charles was nominated by the Marine Corps and left for Houston for his interview. It was several months before Charles heard anything. In May, his wife was about to celebrate her birthday when he received a call saying he had been selected for the second group. Nineteen individuals, including two Europeans, were selected, and Charles was not permitted to share the news with anyone other than his wife. The work had started putting together press releases, etc., so until everything was ready for the announcement, it had to remain a secret. In June 1980, Charles was in Houston training. His first flight came in 1986, and he made a total of four flights. On January 12, they took off for his first flight and landed on the space station on the 18th. In 1986, Charles was the co-pilot for the launch of the Hubble Telescope, and in 1992, he was the commander for the flight, which was a joint U.S. and Russian Cosmonaut mission. As the commander, Charles was responsible for seeing if they could work with the Russians. He reports they bonded well on their mission, and later, President Clinton decided to keep the scientists in the program. They were the first crew to assemble elements of the first space station, and the Russian/American teams have been flying together now for twenty-five years. On January 28, 1986, the space shuttle Challenger broke apart seventy-three seconds into its flight, killing all seven crew members aboard. Charles lost his good friend Ron McNair on that flight when the spacecraft disintegrated 46,000 feet above the Atlantic Ocean, off the coast of Cape Canaveral, Florida. The explosion occurred at 11:39:13 a.m. It was the first fatal accident involving an American spacecraft while in flight. Charles later became the chief of the Safety Division at the Johnson Space Center in Texas, where he oversaw efforts to safely return the shuttle to flight after the Challenger tragedy. In 2009, Charles became the twelfth administrator of the National Aeronautics and Space Administration after being confirmed by the U.S. Senate and having been nominated by President Barack Obama.

What does Charles Bolden Jr. say after sharing his remarkable story? He quickly returns to his time at Drew Park and the Drew Park pool Sharks, highlighting the lifetime and survival skills he developed while a Shark. He vividly recounts the use of the Shepherd's Crook, a pole used to rescue an individual. It's to this writer's sense of emotions he appeals when he discusses how impactful his experience as a Shark so closely resembles the skills he was required to perform throughout his professional life in flight school, as a Marine, and as a United States astronaut flying "pole to pole."

DELANO "DOMINO" BOULWARE

From the outset, there has been a great deal of sharing about the lifeguard experience, particularly as it relates to being a well-paying job. But until now, no one has given the lifeguard position the respect it deserved for the behaviors exhibited. Each lifeguard was a role model to the young swimmers at the Drew Park pool and demanded high standards of behavior in return. The lifeguards were loyal to the young boys and girls and exhibited the highest personal qualities of compassion, caring, and support so valuable to their growth. Their personal responsibility far exceeded saving a life, though they saved lives long after the children were out of the water. When Delano Boulware jumped off the diving board, unable to swim, lifeguard James Evans, or "Foxy" as he was called, rescued him. When the two reached the safety of the pool deck, James asked Delano his name. The response was Delano Boulware, to which James responded, "I'm not going to be able to remember that. I'll just call you Domino, and Domino, I expect to see you here Monday morning at 9:00 a.m., when I'm going to teach you to swim." The nickname Domino from Foxy remains today. Domino was either eight or nine years old that day in 1958 or 1959.

At this point, the writer will briefly stray from Domino's conversation to discuss the use of nicknames. It appeared that many Sharks had nicknames, and some former Sharks indicated they never knew the real names of all the former Sharks who swam on the team. Names like Porky, Granddad, Foxy,

Huck, Pluto, and even Squirt appear throughout, and there were many others. As Grant Lewis shared, the family never used "Foxy" to describe his uncle, though it was fairly common to hear it at the pool. It appeared, as some shared, that a few Sharks had more than one nickname, which at times made it difficult to know which individual was being described as having done something. For this reason, the writer will limit the use of nicknames for accuracy purposes.

Domino reported on one occasion, when the Sharks were going to Jacksonville, Florida, for a swim competition, that he had taken his seat on the bus when he was informed by one of the chaperones that he would have to vacate his seat for another swimmer, who had paid late to go to the competition. Even among the Black community, Domino said there were the "haves and the have-nots" (Saxon Homes "projects" vs. homeowners). Domino did not have the funds to ride the bus to Jacksonville, so the lifeguards had pooled their money to pay his fare. As Domino began to give up his seat on the bus to leave, the lifeguards stepped forward and addressed the chaperone. They politely informed him that if Domino didn't go to Jacksonville, they wouldn't go either. Domino was informed to return to his seat, and he was allowed to go. In a later article written about the trip to Jacksonville, Domino's name was mistakenly omitted. Foxy remained a mentor and a role model for him. The lifeguards at Drew pool made a positive impact daily. They made sure the young boys knew how to read, solve math problems, and to be honest. They could hand out discipline when needed and truly "rescued" the boys for a fulfilling life. To enter the Drew Park pool, swimmers received a hand stamp indicating they had paid their entry fee. It did not take individuals long to learn that with a little water, they could transfer the ink stamp from one hand to another. Even though the shared ink stamp was clearly detectable, lifeguards understood the financial difficulties many young boys and girls faced, so it was not unusual for the lifeguard collecting money at the gate to pretend they did not recognize the fake ink stamp and grant the individual access to the pool. The lifeguards were just that sensitive to the burdens individuals faced, and to the overall positive outcomes of learning to swim and enjoying a fun day.

Delano "Domino" Boulware was born in 1950. He moved to Columbia from Ridgeway, South Carolina, when he was four. He had two brothers and three sisters, and with his mom, the seven members of his family lived in Saxon Homes. Domino's mom was a cook at the State Hospital and raised her children alone. Domino is the second future Shark able to throw a rock from his house and hit the Drew Park pool. Ellis R. Pearson was the first, as you will recall. Once becoming a Shark, Domino practiced with the team each day from 7:00 a.m. to 9:00 a.m., noon to 2:00 p.m., and 6:00 p.m. to 8:00 p.m. The Sharks were a quality swim team, good competitors, and as individuals, generally kept out of trouble. Domino says he now stands up for children because of how he was treated. In his first race, he competed in the 55-yard (50-meter) freestyle, the 55-yard (50-meter) backstroke, and the 55-yard (50-meter) breaststroke. Domino won the blue ribbon in each event, having finished in first place. The team was aware of the times for events completed by the swimmers at Maxcy Gregg. The times were published, and the Sharks could easily compare their times. They knew they were a strong swim team.

Domino, like every other Shark, knew that the Drew pool was led by visionary staff who were "ahead of their time" and the driving force behind the success of Drew Park. Domino credits the staff members for "making him the man he became." He stated they did wonders for him. Domino was certified to be a swim instructor at the age of sixteen. Previously, Domino had served as a junior lifeguard for three years. The pool was run efficiently. A strong, disciplined environment among the lifeguards created a positive, safe, and respectful atmosphere at

Drew Park. "Hard" guys were removed from the Drew pool. The focus was on quality. Lifeguards knew they could easily be replaced if they failed to show up for work, as the list to become a lifeguard far exceeded the number of positions available. When a lifeguard position was not available, extra jobs surfaced. Domino was made aware of a three-week lifeguard stint at a lake in North Carolina. He also learned of a job at a pool in Spartanburg, South Carolina, which gave him the opportunity for employment.

Up to this point in the history of the Drew Park Sharks, the end of the summer competition had primarily been an inter-squad competition. In 1969, the Greenview community opened a pool and established a swimming team. The competition grew into an all-Black city meet, which received extensive coverage in the local newspapers. At a city meet, a coach of the Sharks, known to be very competitive, found one of his team members losing to a member of the Greenview team. In that meet, a female swimmer from Greenview, Domino's future spouse, defeated the young woman from the Sharks' team. To date, that coach has yet to present his wife with her first-place trophy, and it still bothers him that his swimmer lost the race.

The reader will shortly read about the Sunday lifeguard water show at Drew pool. Domino shared that the event generally included a "ring of fire" performance, acrobatic diving, and more. The water show was truly an amazing event, loved by the nearly 1,000 attendees. The nearby town of Irmo would bus people to the pool. Domino also played baseball in the summer. One summer day, Domino had a swim meet and a baseball game scheduled at the same time. Domino swam a couple of events, but when he needed to be at the ballpark, he left the pool. Over the loudspeaker, Domino heard, "Swimmers report to the starting block." He missed that event due to the game. To this day, he's surprised no action was taken toward him. The lessons Domino learned have remained ingrained in his mind these many years.

The writer has already mentioned that Domino has always stood up for children because of the behavior he experienced at the Drew Park pool. He tells kids, "You have to get it wrong sometimes before you get it right," and that judges want you "on this side of the court" when he talks to them while giving tennis lessons. In 1975, Domino saw Arthur Ashe win a tennis match. He was inspired. He learned to play, and for the past forty years, he has been teaching tennis at Greenview Park. He started the Bolden/Martin Tennis Camp for Math and Science. It is a free camp. Today, Domino is the tennis pro/instructor at Greenview Tennis Center. He was elected to the South Carolina Tennis Hall of Fame in 2017.

After high school, Domino went to Benedict College. He had been asked by Coach Bradley to attend South Carolina State University. He left Benedict, following his first year. He spent six months in California but left rather quickly following a large earthquake. Looking for employment, Domino found two options. One was at the Columbia Corrections Institute (prison), but after walking the halls and going through so many locked doors, he determined that job probably didn't suit him. His next job interview found him behind the camera as a cameraman for television news. Mr. Rudolph Canzater conducted that interview. With no experience, he found himself at WNOK, which later became WLTX. He became the director for newscasts for the 6:00 a.m., noon, and evening news. He received extensive on-the-job training. He later worked for twenty-nine years at ETV and spent eight years in Beaufort, South Carolina. Domino shared that he once spent a week in this writer's hometown, Zanesville, Ohio, reporting on the school system there. That was genuinely an unexpected tale to hear.

TONY THOMAS

This writer thought he was becoming somewhat complacent and wasn't convinced he would hear much new and exciting material, unlike from others who had shared previously. Tony Thomas proved him wrong. This writer continues to be astounded at the lives of the Drew Park Sharks. They have far exceeded all expectations and remain fascinating stories. Born in Columbia in 1952 to a father stationed at Fort Jackson and a mother who served as a clerk, Tony lived in the Greenview community. Greenview was the first community planned in conjunction with the city of Columbia and Fort Jackson, as a community for Black soldiers. Fort Jackson was the number one training base in the United States. As a young boy, Tony saw Bruce Lee on the big screen, and from that moment on, he became an ardent fan, to say the least, of karate. This writer will not detail Tony's lifetime love of karate at this point, but you will soon discover just how impactful Bruce Lee became to him.

Tony started swimming at Drew pool around the age of thirteen. As his mother worked, she was able to drop him off on occasion. Tony relayed that the city buses did not go to Harden Street, near Drew Park, so on many days, he and a small group of his friends would "thumb" their way to the pool. He indicated that it was not unusual for a man or woman driving alone in their car to pick up the small group and give them a ride. The group would generally get a ride from Greenview to Beltline Blvd and then thumb an additional ride to Harden Street. There were days Tony and his friends walked to the Drew pool. When it was time to return home, they used the method that had worked to get them to the pool: their thumbs. Their small group included both boys and girls, all young teens.

Like Ellis Pearson, Tony was a self-taught swimmer. He had the unique ability to watch others swim and learned by mimicking what he had seen. He used the same technique for learning to dive. The Drew pool had four diving boards. Two of the springboards were 1-meter boards, and two were 3-meter boards. As you, the reader, will quickly learn, diving became Tony's passport for his future travels. Tony was a competitor for the Sharks, and his favorite stroke was the breaststroke. In addition, he swam distances, including the 500 and 1,000. Though not included as an event in any Drew Park Sharks' competitive swim meet, Tony loved diving. He learned from some of the best, in his opinion, at Drew, including Howard "Porky" Simmons and Delano "Domino" Boulware. As noted earlier, it appeared everyone had a nickname. Tony's was Huck, though he said few people called him by that name. While this writer was with Tony, he called Domino with a question and called him Domino on the phone. It certainly appears nicknames have a way of sticking with you forever. Getting back to diving, this writer is talking some serious diving. This was just not going to the end of the board and performing a beautiful swan dive. We're talking a one and one-and-a-half flip in either the tuck or pike position. We're talking about a two-and-one-half in the tuck or pike position. Tony would do a one or one-and-a-half with a full twist or the reverse dive, commonly called a gainer. In diving, a gainer is a backward somersault while moving forward, rather than backward off a springboard or platform. Basically, you walk to the end of the board, spring up, and do a backward flip toward the board from which you just sprang. As the reader can clearly see, Tony performed a variety of competitive dives. Tony shared that at the beginning of his dive training, he wore a T-shirt because the water tended to sting if the dive was not performed correctly.

While still in high school (1969), the Greenview community opened a 25-meter swimming pool. Tony, then sixteen, swam at both the Drew Park and Greenview pools. He shared that he believed Drew Park actually had had two pools prior to the opening of the current Drew Park Wellness Center. He thinks the first Drew Park pool was aligned north-south, while the second pool, upon renovation, was aligned east-west in the park. This writer learned that a second pool was built following the demolition of the original pool. This occurred in the late 1980s, and the pool differed from the original. As most others have shared, Drew Park was an outstanding facility for African Americans throughout the community and the area. Tony indicated it was not unusual for the pool to have 900 to 1,000 "swimmers" on any given Sunday. The word "swimmers" is in quotation marks because Tony indicated that many pool participants were unable to swim. Tony, like many of his Shark friends, became a lifeguard. He began as a junior lifeguard before becoming a certified lifeguard. He earned his senior lifesaving certificate in his senior year of high school and began working as a lifeguard at the Drew pool. Like several of his peers, Tony was water safety instructor certified, which allowed him to give swimming lessons. The pool at Drew Park was closed for two to three hours on the days of competition and opened later, though in earlier years it closed the entire day of Saturday meets. There was just no way to hold a swim meet with the pool's regular attendance on any given day. While some Sharks noted they played football in high school, Tony was a member of his high school track team. He was primarily a distance runner (the mile and the half mile) and a high jumper, but he also ran the 180-yard low hurdles and finished third in the State track meet in that event.

It should come as no surprise that, upon graduating from high school, Tony was awarded a four-year scholarship to South Carolina State University, where he was both a swimmer and a diver. Tony was the first Drew Park Shark and Greenview Park swimmer to earn a diving scholarship and dive competitively at the college level. He was a member of the swim team all four years. As a diver, Tony qualified for the Nationals three out of the four years he was at South Carolina State University, based on his diving scores. He could have competed nationally if he had wanted to, but he chose not to compete at that level for personal reasons and settled for comparing his diving scores from his meets to those set nationally. In 2021, Tony was inducted into the South Carolina State University "Athlete Hall of Fame."

Early on, the reader learned about Tony's interest in karate after seeing Bruce Lee in *The Green Hornet*. Tony identified with Bruce Lee, as he was smaller, like Tony. At Fairwall Junior High School, where Tony attended, his physical education teacher sponsored after-school activities to give students things to do. Tony's friends were also interested in karate, and the group bought books and practiced karate moves. Tony's English teacher had a black belt in judo, which he had earned while being stationed in Korea during the war. Tony and his friends began earning belts from the lessons he gave, and he continued through high school, working out three or four times a week. By the time Tony completed high school, he had earned his brown belt.

While a freshman at South Carolina State University, Tony met another first-year student from Charleston who, like him, was a brown belt in karate. Tony had been involved in karate for most of his early years. The two began working out together, and increasingly, other students watched them with growing interest. They started the Bulldog Karate Club, which became the largest student organization at South Carolina State

University. Tony earned his black belt in karate in 1971. Still a college student, Tony competed in karate meets throughout the Southeast. In 1973, at a meet being held in Charleston, South Carolina, Tony fought Bill Wallace, the number one fighter in the United States. Bill Wallace later became Elvis Presley's bodyguard. ESPN has a TV program featuring Bill Wallace and Elvis, available online. Though Elvis had a karate instructor, he also learned moves from Bill Wallace. In performances, one can see Elvis performing karate kicks while singing. Tony estimates the Bulldog Karate Club taught 300 students while at South Carolina State University.

Tony graduated with a degree in education. He taught physical education for the next thirty-nine years, mostly in District 1 in Columbia, except for a two-year stint in Newberry. He often had demonstrations for his elementary-aged students by the Karate Club members. During the summer months, Tony continued to work at the Drew pool, where he served as assistant manager. He supervised lifeguards, monitored rotations and the basket room, and counted money for bank deposits. The cost to swim was around fifty cents unless you were very young, and then it was twenty-five cents. Tony continued competing in tournaments while a teacher, and in 1997, he opened the Tony Thomas Karate School in Columbia. He has been in business in Columbia for the past twenty-nine years and at his current location for nineteen of those years. The walls of his karate studio are filled with photographs of former students from their early beginnings. He said that many have grown, returned with their children to learn, and earned their black belts under him. In all, Tony estimates he has taught over 15,000 students. He has been inducted into several Karate Halls of Fame during his fifty-nine total years of karate. He is a tenth-degree black belt. Tony met his wife at a karate competition, and she has a black belt in karate. Tony said he had not taught her every trick he knows!

GARY E. BELL, DOCTOR OF HEALTH ADMINISTRATION (DHA)

Like most of the Sharks before him, Gary Bell's venture into swimming came because of his mother wanting him to learn to swim, so she took him to the Drew pool each day for swim lessons. The involvement of parents has been a recurring theme in these individual stories, so we begin by paying homage to them for their instrumental role in their success. Gary was about seven or eight when he first began to swim. Born in Columbia in 1946, Gary lived in Allen Benedict Court, or, as he refers to it, the projects. In some locales, the term "projects" might be interpreted as a negative descriptor for a living environment, but for Gary, it was a term of endearment. In his mind, Allen Benedict Court was the place to be. This was reinforced to this writer by a friend and colleague, Eartha Jones, who indicated her grandmother had once lived in Allen Benedict Court. In the conversation, Eartha reinforced how appealing the community was, with its well-maintained homes and positive community. You will recall that Ellis Pearson mowed lawns for Saxon Homes residents to earn money to pay his pool fee, as the two communities were very near.

Gary learned to swim from several of the lifeguards. As a member of the Midget Boys, Gary swam freestyle. It was a stroke he enjoyed swimming. He swam the 55-yard (50-meter) and 100-meter freestyle. Maybe more so than anyone this writer has met, for Gary, swimming became a real lifetime passion, which you will read about later. Gary liked competing at swim meets and shared that at one meet in Augusta, the relay team was behind when the second leg touched the wall. He caught up during the third leg of the relay and passed his opponents so that he touched the wall leading. He turned over the final leg to Talmadge Dixon, who brought home the victory in his typical outstanding manner. Gary shared that he and Robert Bradley, the future swim coach at South Carolina State University, were swim mates on the Sharks' team. They swam together as well in the Palmetto Games. Gary was a middle-distance swimmer, but he always wished to challenge Robert, known as Pluto, in the shorter distances. After getting beaten soundly by "Pluto" in a meet held at Johnson C. Smith University, Gary decided to remain a middle-distance swimmer.

Gary became a lifeguard at Drew pool after passing his required certification. Prior to becoming a lifeguard and actually sitting in the chair, Gary was a junior lifeguard. Gary wasn't totally sure the title "junior lifeguard" was an actual position, but each morning he was there when the pool opened, selling and collecting tickets, cleaning, making sure the showers had soap and the bathrooms had tissue, and closing at night. Gary noted his godparents, the Fair family, ran the snack bar at Drew Park.

Like several other members of the swim team, Gary played football in high school at C.A. Johnson High School, and he found the Drew pool staff willing to support this endeavor. Talking about the staff at Drew, Gary said the group was made up of quality men who were just good men. Gary and the other lifeguards would send a note of appreciation to the staff at the end of the summer to specify their intentions for the next summer. As noted previously, a veteran lifeguard was re-hired to his position each summer for as long as he wanted it. Gary worked as a lifeguard every summer while he was in high school. He worked the summers following high school if his schedule permitted. Upon graduation, Gary attended South Carolina State University and was a member of the freshman swim team. While at South Carolina State University, he joined Omega Psi Phi Fraternity, Inc. At South Carolina State University, freshmen and sophomores were required to take ROTC classes. In Gary's junior year, he enrolled in Advanced ROTC, and upon graduation the next year, Gary was commissioned a Second Lieutenant in the Army. Gary served in the Army for three-and-a-half years and completed one tour of duty in Vietnam. He returned to the States and was assigned to several military bases before ending his army career at Fort Jackson.

Upon his return to Columbia, Gary began working at Benedict College as the assistant director for business affairs. He had an undergraduate degree in mathematics with a minor in accounting. At Benedict College, his supervisor was previously his accounting professor. Gary decided he wanted to be an accountant and needed a master's degree in accounting. He enrolled at Kent State University in Kent, Ohio, where he earned his Master of Science in Accounting Degree in eighteen months, followed by a Master of Business Administration from Winthrop University in South Carolina. He passed the CPA exam and became an employee of one of the Big Eight accounting firms, Arthur Andersen & Co. He worked in Charlotte, Columbia, and Atlanta before deciding to return to Columbia. Upon his return to Columbia, Gary assumed the position of deputy director at the South Carolina Department of Social Services, a position he held for nearly fourteen years. He also served as vice president for business affairs at Florence-Darlington Technical College and as deputy director for fiscal management and information systems at the South Carolina Department of Health and Human Services. While at Health and Human Services, Gary earned a Doctor of Health

Administration (DHA) degree from the Medical University of South Carolina.

Early in this writer's meeting with Gary, he emphasized he "loved immensely" his time at the pool and swimming. He never lost that feeling. Upon his return to Columbia, Gary became a registered Master's Class swimmer. He competed in Masters swim meets across the Carolinas and usually swam ten events during the two days of competition. Gary swam all the strokes at the 50 and 100-meter distances, and he swam the 100 individual and 200 individual medleys. The medley consists of the swimmer doing all four strokes (in order): the butterfly, the backstroke, the breaststroke, and the freestyle. Gary gave up swimming Masters in 2020, around the time of the COVID pandemic. As noted near the beginning of this article, swimming has many health benefits, and Gary, more than any other former Shark, felt that swimming was an excellent activity for maintaining a healthy lifestyle as he grew older. Again, research has proven this as fact. Gary set a personal goal to swim 300 miles in one year. Clearly, that's about a mile a day for almost an entire year. The next year, Gary increased his goal to swim 400 miles. Not willing to stop there, his next year's goal was 500 miles, and finally, his fourth year's goal was to swim 600 miles. Gary accomplished every one of his personal goals. He stated he completed the 600-mile goal on December 3 of the fourth year. For the remainder of that month, Gary swam 13 miles. He decided, though, that as he got older, swimming longer distances was probably something most people did not need to do to remain healthy. Gary currently swims at Drew pool three days a week for a mile and a half. He ran Masters track, but following multiple knee surgeries, he quit running. Another reason to be a swimmer is the physiological benefits.

Gary shared some thoughts briefly on being a member of an all-Black swim team. He wished the Sharks could have competed against the team at Maxcy Gregg. He felt confident they could have won. Those feelings were duplicated as he felt the same about his high school football team. He was proud of his high school, citing that he had four choices for foreign languages, including Latin, French, German, and Spanish. Gary chose German in high school. He felt confident that few other nearby schools offered so many choices. Integration was not an end-all for Gary. He wanted new schoolbooks, not used hand-me-downs from the white schools when they got new ones. As for Plessy, Gary just wanted "equal."

He attended the funeral of a friend a year ago. Following the service, he was introduced by a friend to a man who had recently returned to Columbia after living in California for many years. Upon hearing his name, the man said, "Gary Bell, you were a lifeguard at the Drew Park pool, and you taught me to swim." It made Gary proud, and he commented that his experiences at Drew pool had impacted lives beyond his imagination. Through the phone, this writer could sense his smile.

STEPHEN MCINTOSH

For this writer, this is a first: a conversation with two members of the same family swimming on the Drew Park Pool Sharks team. I am aware, though, that this is not the only family with multiple members who become Sharks. You have already read that Jimmie Ruff had two children on the team: April and JR. There is at least one family, the Andersons, with three siblings who swam, and one family, the Harkness family, with four sons (Mark, Tim, Kip, and George) who swam on the team. The names of other families with at least two members on the swim team included: Bolden, Brandyburg, Kearse, McIntosh, Bell, Kennedy, and several others.

Stephen McIntosh joined his brother, Stanley, for swim lessons around the age of nine or ten. They would be dropped off each morning by their mother at approximately 8:30 a.m. each day for lessons, which began at 9:00. They, like others, started in the "beginners" class. Swim lessons generally lasted approximately an hour, where the focus of the instructors (lifeguards) was being comfortable putting your head under water, learning to float, learning to glide through the water, and basic strokes. After swimming lessons, the boys spent the remainder of the morning "swimming" until their mom picked them up around noon. Something, though, was uniquely different about the McIntosh boys. It was apparent from the beginning that these two had a knack for swimming. It seemed to come easily to them, and they learned quickly. So much so that by their second summer, they were already in the intermediate class, and the instructors were using them to help teach the very large beginner classes at Drew pool. Generally, from the beginner class, one moved to the advanced beginner class, followed by the intermediate class. As members of the intermediate swim class, the boys focused on refining their strokes.

Stephen was only thirteen months behind Stanley, as he was born in 1957. Unlike Stanley, who was born in Germany while his father was serving in the military, Stephen was born at Fort Jackson.

As most others have noted, Stephen praised all the staff members, coaches, and lifeguards, who together created the driving force behind Drew Park, the swim team, the pool in general, and the atmosphere of success among African Americans during this period. They were instrumental in promoting water safety, and they established an avenue for young men and women to create opportunities that benefited them throughout their lives. One such opportunity was employment as a lifeguard with a water safety certification. At the age of fifteen, when Stanley was attending the water safety instructor class, Stephen was told to take the course as well. Stephen was informed it would be a good experience for him, even though he would take the class for a second time the following year. The next year, Stephen passed the class and became a lifeguard, a position he held for three years during high school. Stephen had fond memories of his time with the Sharks. During competitions, he sometimes swam the backstroke, but he was best known as a strong freestyle competitor.

More so than anyone thus far, Stephen chose to share the daily routine of the lifeguards at Drew Park pool. The lifeguards generally worked the entire summer and even began working during the final week of the school year, preparing the pool for opening day of the summer. The pool was open every day of the week. There were three lifeguard chairs at the pool. Two chairs were located nearer the middle of the pool, where both the shallow and middle depth could be observed, and one chair in the deep end near the diving boards. As noted previously, the shallow end was approximately three feet deep, the middle section five or six feet deep, and the deep end was twelve feet deep. Two lifeguards worked in half-hour shifts while one was on break. Following the break, lifeguards would rotate chairs. Stephen recalled that swim practice often took place during lunchtime at the pool. On Monday through Friday, the first shift of lifeguards ended around 2:30 or 3:00 p.m., and the second shift of lifeguards began and worked until approximately 8:00 p.m. Stephen indicated they generally left the pool around 8:30 p.m. if they had worked the afternoon shift. In addition to the six full-time lifeguards employed each summer to monitor swimmers, a seventh lifeguard was responsible for maintaining the pool and was known as the pool engineer. Saturday's work began with the cleaning of the pool. The morning shift lifeguards would begin in the shallow end, sweeping debris into the deep end of the pool with brooms. Once they reached the deep end, they would use vacuums powered by a generator to remove the debris. The pool had two large filters in the deepest end, near the diving boards, used for filtration. Sundays at Drew Park were the busiest days. The pool opened later in the day, around noon, generally following church time. All six lifeguards worked on Sundays, with all three lifeguard chairs occupied and one additional lifeguard walking the pool deck in the shallow end. Again, there have been previous remarks about the Sundays at Drew Park. The park was like vacation time for many African Americans from communities near and far. Spots would be claimed on the bleachers and towels laid out, for plans to spend the entire day.

In reflection, Stephen said being a Shark made him so proud. He said he didn't really appreciate the experience and its significance to him until later in life. After all, he had become a proficient swimmer and had obtained a job as a lifeguard, which was both well-paying and just a great job, period. Stephen said it made him proud to be known by so many, as he interacted with a huge number of the area's citizens.

Following high school graduation, Stephen attended South Carolina State University. Stephen was academically driven, and he had plans for his future. Those plans did not allow room for swimming. He had several conversations with his brother, Stanley, who had enrolled a year earlier and was on the swim team. They both agreed that the time needed to be a member of the swim team would be more time-consuming than Stephen preferred. He majored in political science with an emphasis on pre-law. Upon graduation, Stephen entered The Ohio State University School of Law. After receiving his law degree, he practiced law in the city prosecutor's office and later became chief prosecutor in Columbus, Ohio. As of this writing, Stephen has completed nineteen years as a judge in the Common Pleas Court, dealing with both felonies and civil cases from rape and murder to lawsuits over wrongful deaths and contract disputes. Stephen and his wife have three children, and each learned to swim. Two have served as lifeguards, like their father. This writer will note that one of Stephen's sons graduated from Ohio University, the alma mater of this writer. (Go Bobcats!)

MOSES HOPKINS

1934 – AUGUST 2024

AS SHARED BY HIS CHILDREN,
ANNETTE HOPKINS MCCOY AND ANTHONY HOPKINS

f you were to look up the word "athlete" in the Merriam-Webster Dictionary, you might just see a photograph of Moses Hopkins. To the extent that most people have athletic talent in one sport, Moses Hopkins excelled as a swimmer, football player, golfer, tennis player, and cliff diver in the Bahamas. He also enjoyed bowling and skating—roller skating, not ice skating. This writer still owns his ice skates from his youth in Ohio. Born to a family of entrepreneurs, business owners, college graduates, educators, and sports enthusiasts, Moses Hopkins lived an extraordinary life. Born in 1934, the family lived in the Waverly Community near Pine Street. He later moved to Allen Benedict Court before Saxon Homes was constructed. His final move was to Laurel Street, where he lived most of his lifetime. His parents were both college graduates. His mother was a graduate of Allen University, his father from Benedict College. His mom was eighteen hours into a PhD program. She retired as an educator, and Moses' father retired as a state employee. They owned a restaurant called Hops Spaghetti House on Gervais Street. Moses' nickname was Hops as well. Moses' father was also an athlete. As the story goes, while a child, Moses's father taught him to swim by telling him to "get out of the boat" on Lake Murray, with instructions to swim back to shore. Having heard that tale, Moses' mom was adamant that the story would never be repeated, and she would see her son learn to swim properly. Moses attended Camp Atwater in Massachusetts at the age of ten, where he learned to swim. Camp Atwater, established in 1921, was the oldest Black-owned camp in the United States. He may well have attended Atwater with his best childhood and lifetime friend, Rupert Brown. Moses and Rupert were in each other's weddings, and their moms shared a birthday.

Moses was among the first to swim at the Drew Park pool when it opened in 1950. He had moved to Allen Benedict Court, which was within walking distance of the pool. Moses became one of the first lifeguards at the Drew Park pool. Moses swam the breaststroke and was nothing short of a phenom. There were trophies at Drew Park to prove his excellence. The breaststroke was not only his favorite stroke but also one he excelled in, and his time in the breaststroke was just six seconds off the world record. As a swim instructor, Moses taught many future city leaders, pool staff, and others to swim.

Annette reports that Moses met his future wife in high school, where they dated. Moses played football, and Margret was a majorette. Moses taught her to swim. Like Moses, she was certified in water safety, though she was not as fond of the water as Moses. After high school, her mom stayed near her home and attended Allen University. She later taught physical education and dance. With a swimming scholarship in his hands, Moses went to South Carolina State University for his freshman year. After the first year of swimming at South Carolina State University, his swimming coach left for Fisk University, wanting Moses to follow him there. Moses decided to attend Morehouse College and swim. Still dating Margaret, Moses decided he would transfer, for his senior year, to Allen University to be near her. Moses, too, majored in and taught physical education. Moses worked for the South Carolina Red Cross delivering blood. He was frequently called when a drowning occurred at Lake Murray to retrieve the body. He taught Red Cross training for the students at Allen University. He later worked for the Bethlehem Center, managing youth recreation, and for the Columbia Housing Authority. Moses retired from the Department of Juvenile Justice, again managing the recreation program, and he frequently took the youth to the Drew pool for swimming.

Moses and Margaret were the parents of two children, Annette and Anthony. Unlike his father, Anthony stated he was nearly "afraid" of the water. Annette stated that once Anthony "fell into the water" and was seen rapidly "walking on the water" to escape. Even if swimming wasn't Anthony's sport, he enjoyed playing football and tennis. Anthony had seven children. He has twenty grandchildren. Moses taught his grandchildren to swim. Annette became Dr. Annette Hopkins McCoy, with a PhD in management. She owns a business and serves as a manager for a nonprofit. She resides in the family home on Laurel Street today. Annette learned to swim, though she was never a lifeguard like her father. She indicated she liked the water and began swimming in elementary school. At the age of sixteen, Annette graduated from high school with her heart set on attending The Ohio State University. With some gentle persuasion, Annette decided on Talladega College, an HBCU institution in Alabama. She met a man while in college and suggested to her mom that she might transfer from her institution. Having been an active participant in a similar transfer situation as a college student, her mom strongly encouraged her not to do so.

Annette repeated what has become common knowledge to the readers: Drew Park and the pool were iconic and one of the best features known in Columbia. Like so many others, Annette said one would rise in the morning, pack a lunch, and head to the pool for the entire day, staying even until dusk. She said everyone knew everyone. The pool was surrounded by a high fence, and parents could stand outside to watch their children. It was simply a great set-up, she noted. There were separate entrances for boys and girls, and a community center just down from the pool that offered after-school programs and adult activities, and some have reported even attending kindergarten there. The infamous sprinklers were also outside the pool's fence, which so many have praised. Amidst all of this was Moses Hopkins. Annette said, "Daddy was Drew Park." She said the "worst thing to ever happen was to tear down the Drew Park pool." It had always been well maintained, and clearly the best pool around. The deep twelve-foot section of the pool, with the diving boards, was virtually impossible to replace for the community. For this reason, you will understand why Stanley McIntosh strongly supports the city developing an outstanding aquatic center. Stanley, with the support of Moses Hopkins, was an invaluable ambassador to the sport of swimming, leading young competitors annually in the U.S. Youth Games across the United States. It has always been, and continues to be, Stanley's dream for the city to have a complex that would rival any in the U.S. The reader will recall that Stanley first became aware of such programs and facilities during his freshman year as a swimmer at South Carolina State University. At her father's funeral service, Annette said she finally fully realized the value, the extent, and the impact Moses had made on others throughout his years and his service to the many people of Columbia. He genuinely was Drew Park.

THADDEUS BELL, MD

The reader will recognize the last name of this member of the Drew Park Sharks, as Gary Bell shared his story earlier. Thaddeus is the older brother, born in 1944, two years earlier. The Bell family had two additional members, a sister, Veta, and a brother, Reginald. They were not members of the Drew Park Sharks. As you will recall, the family lived in Allen Benedict Court. Their father was a professional barber with a shop near Pine and Taylor Streets, between Allen University and Benedict College. Thad's father's name was John Hamilton "Jim" Bell, and he had numerous professional clients. The president of South Carolina State University was a weekly client, as were many professionals from the nearby universities and from throughout the city. Thad said his dad taught the family that your word should be your "bond." He felt that if your head and shoes were well-groomed, you were a person of good character. When Thad's father was in conversation with someone getting a haircut, and the man used a word his father was unfamiliar with, he would ask his client to use the word again and possibly even spell it. Later, his dad would be found searching the word in the dictionary, so the word could then become a part of his vocabulary. He frequently had a list of words he had developed from conversations.

Thad's mom was a schoolteacher. She had graduated from Allen University around 1938 and was "Miss Allen" while in college. She taught special education. She was fond of poems, and she made her children learn poems such as "Somebody's Mother," "House With Nobody In It," and "If." Thaddeus reflects on many of the poems he learned even today, and he has a deep appreciation for having learned them. He finds they have created an interesting awareness for his life and caused him to come "full circle" as he considers life and the lives of those he meets. His mother often quoted from the poem "The House by the Side of the Road." Thaddeus said his mother had a reputation for stopping her car while driving down the road if she saw an item she could pick up, clean, and give away to someone in need. Thaddeus indicated their backyard often looked like a junkyard. If she saw an old refrigerator along the side of the road, she would order the boys to go pick it up and bring it home. She often washed old clothes no longer wanted by others and gave them away. One day, Thaddeus was taking his mother to visit her sister in Washington, DC, and while having her driver's license examined at the airport, the security woman exclaimed, "Are you the Ms. Hattie Bell who taught school in Fairfield County Schools? Oh my god, you'll never remember, but you used to give my mother clean clothes for us to wear." Thaddeus says even today, while browsing Facebook, he will get a comment from someone his mother helped at some point in the past.

As both Gary and Thaddeus reported, their mother took them to the pool each day so they could learn to swim. She wanted them to have a good experience. He was thirteen or fourteen years old when he went to the pool for the first time. He played Little League Baseball, not 200 yards from the pool. Thaddeus became a lifeguard like his brother. When they would need to report to work early in the morning, before either had time for breakfast, their mother would cook them breakfast and bring it to them at the pool. Charles Bolden, Sr., was a mentor to Thad. Bolden was the manager of the Drew pool and hired Thad to be a lifeguard at sixteen. Thaddeus became water safety certified at age eighteen. A Water Safety Instructor was the Red Cross program that certified the individual as competent in the nine strokes of swimming, proficient in lifesaving, and qualified to teach others to be lifeguards. As for Drew pool swimming competitions, Thaddeus indicated he didn't excel like so many others. He said he didn't see it as his forte.

With such strong competition for summer lifeguard jobs, as noted throughout various individual stories, Thad, with the support of the leadership team at Drew, found employment at a Girl Scout Camp. Bethlehem Center Girl Scout Camp was run by the Methodist Church located in North Carolina. The camp had a lake, and Thad, along with one of his friends, David Whaley, elected to work as lifeguards there. As the camp was well into the woods, the boys used their spare time to get into shape for football season. Charles Bolden, Sr. was, in addition, the football coach at C.A. Johnson High School. David Whaley was the captain of the high school team. On the first play, in the first game of the season that fall, David experienced an injury that would alter both his and Thad's lives. On that first play of the game, David was hit in the left side of his body, rupturing his spleen. It was 1961 or 1962, and there was no EMS one could call for support. Instead, a local funeral home hearse transported David to Waverly Hospital for emergency surgery. Dr. Everett L. Dargan, a young and promising surgeon with a growing and successful practice, operated on David and removed his spleen. Thad and his friends went to visit David on Saturday morning. Thad said David had tubes sticking in various parts of his body. While visiting, Dr. Dargan was completing rounds. Thad began asking questions about David's recovery, ability to play football, and the procedure. Thad admits that he didn't have any idea what the spleen was or what its purpose was to the human body. He found Dr. Dargan's knowledge fascinating, and at that moment, it was like a lightning bolt striking. Thad knew he wanted to become a doctor. Today, Thaddeus Bell is Dr. Thaddeus Bell. David recovered and returned to high school. Thad nicknamed him Spleen. That year, the football team won the AAA Football State Championship by defeating Howard High School. Each member of the team received a football jacket. Due to a state high school regulation, David, the team's captain, could not receive a jacket because he had not played sixteen quarters, the minimum required to be awarded one. After all, he had been injured on the first play of the first game of the season. Unbeknownst to Thad, David carried this disappointment of feeling he was not part of the team for more than fifty years. At a funeral for one of their friends, Thad was asked to deliver a eulogy. He called some of his friends for any details about Hugh that he might include in the eulogy. While talking to some of his former high school teammates, he was not only reminded that his friend generally offered a prayer before leaving the locker room but also that David had always felt bad about not getting a football jacket. Following a conversation with the deceased's family, Thad arranged to present David with a jacket after delivering his eulogy. Needless to say, David was overwhelmed at the ceremony, and Thad felt it had finally closed the loop on the football issue. The framed football jacket is currently a part of the C.A. Johnson Hall of Fame display.

While in high school, Thad spent his football off-season studying science and working on science projects. He entered the South Carolina Science Fair and placed first. He got to represent C.A. Johnson High School and the State of South Carolina in Seattle, Washington, at the National/International Science Fair, held in conjunction with the 1962 World's Fair. The World's Fair was officially called the Century 21 Exposition, and the Space Needle and the ALWEG monorail had their debut. Thad was one of the first people to travel to the top of the Space Needle and ride the monorail. Marshall

Parks was a football coach and advisor to the Science Fair. There were two Science Fairs of South Carolina, one for each race. Thad said he never met the winner of the white science fair. As a high school senior, Thad was interested in microbiology and took courses at Benedict College.

Thad had two out-of-state football scholarship offers, but the scholarships weren't full, and his father didn't feel either was enough to justify going out of state. He hoped Thad would attend South Carolina State University. Thad had received a work-aid (work-study) scholarship for four years as a lab assistant in microbiology at South Carolina State University. Thad heard the football team was starting early, so he left early for college with the intent of making the team. Thad tried out for the team and won a scholarship to play. The president of the campus, while getting his haircut from Thad's dad, mentioned that Thad made the football team, prompting a call from his dad. His dad was concerned he might get hurt and informed Thad, "You won't get hurt in the lab." He also told him that he needed to do as he was told, or he could stay somewhere else. Thad's dad was not impressed with athletes, but he was impressed with Black men who were educated. Thad decided to quit the football team.

Thad attended South Carolina State University and swam his freshman year. He swam the 50-meter breaststroke, but as with his previous swimming experiences, he felt he was just not good enough, and he didn't win any medals. Because Thad was a college swimmer and had been a Drew Park Shark, when the Department of the Interior was searching for swimmers to recommend for the position of park ranger, Thad was selected as one of the first African Americans to receive the prestigious summer job. He spent three summers at Yosemite National Park in California. The National Park Service was a part of the Department of the Interior. He was almost ready to be a permanent Ranger when he learned he might be drafted into the Army. The Registrar at South Carolina State University notified his parents that he was on the draft list. Following a conversation with his parents, he decided he could avoid the draft by becoming a teacher. The South Carolina Teachers' Association wanted to integrate schools, and Thad was recommended to be one of the first African American teachers at a white high school. The superintendent of the Cherokee County Schools at Gaffney High School called, and Thad accepted a job. Gaffney had a reputation as a racist community, but Thad went to work and had an amazing experience. In the beginning, white students wanted to get out of his classes, but soon there were so many students wanting to get into his classes that he was told to stop making promises about entry, as there just wasn't enough room. After the first year, Thad moved to Charleston with a strong recommendation from his Cherokee County superintendent, and he became the first African American teacher at Charleston High School.

One event did occur while Thad was a student at South Carolina State University. He was part of 700 men from his college dorm who were arrested while protesting and marching at a bowling alley for being denied entry. The Selma Bridge March had just recently ended. The entire group was sent to the Correctional Institute in Columbia, and the group was kept locked up for two weeks. Civil rights attorney Mathew Perry represented the group of protesters. The event occurred during Thad's sophomore year.

After teaching for five years, Thaddeus went to Atlanta University for his master's degree. He had been turned down twice for medical school and, after receiving his master's degree, applied again to the Medical School of South Carolina. The medical school was not accepting applications from African American candidates. He accepted a job at St. Andrews High School, a historically white school that had integrated. The father of one of his students was the associate director at the medical school, and he informed Thad that the federal government was going to be taking away funds if African Americans were continually barred from entry. Thad applied and was accepted to medical school in 1972. In 1976, he graduated. Upon graduation, Thad enlisted in the Air Force. Stationed in Charleston, Thad, a major, became a flight surgeon, which certified pilots for the qualifications to fly. He served in the Air Force until 1991 following Operation Desert Storm. In 1993, Thad was appointed to his first of two prestigious positions with the medical school. He became the associate dean of students of the College of Medicine, where he served from 1993 to 2004. Simultaneously, Thad was the director of diversity for the Medical College from 1996 to 2000.

One day, Thad was seen running, and the individual informed him he should consider competing in the Masters Track and Field competitions. Thad became the only former Shark to become a world champion in Masters Track and Field (100-meter dash, age 40–44 and 45–49) from South Carolina. He holds all the Master's records in sprinting in the 40–50-year age group and was on three 4x100 world championship relay teams. He was a two-time world champion in the 100- and 400-meter dashes at the medical games. The *Post and Courier News Paper* selected him as one of the best athletes of the twentieth century in South Carolina. Dr. Thaddeus Bell is being considered for the South Carolina Hall of Fame. After practicing medicine for the past forty-eight years, he continues to work as a family physician in Charleston. This year, Dr. Thaddeus Bell will receive his sixty-year pin from his fraternity, Omega Psi Phi, Inc., for dedicated service to the fraternity.

DR. HARVEY DORRAH, PHD

To share any story about Harvey Dorrah, one must begin with the role that Jimmie Ruff played in his life. Harvey credits Jimmie for keeping his life on course, teaching him to swim, recognizing his potential, and for his efforts to help him be involved in the lives of children. Like Ellis Pearson, Harvey was selected to work with younger children learning to swim. He specifically noted helping Ellis's little brother, Birdie, in his journey to become a swimmer. Born in 1951, Harvey initially lived near Booker T. Washington High School before moving to Allen-Benedict Court. His mother began in Columbia doing domestic work before obtaining a position at Fort Jackson, where she was employed as a clerk in the stock room, and later in the military store. Harvey was eight or nine years old when his mom's fiancé invited him to join him at Drew pool. The Drew pool became Harvey's "hangout." With one of his friends, they shared a paper route and often went to the pool together. Harvey entered the junior lifeguard program, and he passed all training requirements. Harvey was asked—very encouragingly, he adds—to participate in the senior lifeguard training and was informed by the staff member that Harvey "must" get his Water Safety Instructor certification. At eighteen, as a college freshman after graduating from C.A. Johnson High School, Harvey began his WSI certification. It was during his certification that Harvey earned his nickname. During one aspect of the certification exercises, it was heard, "Come on, Granddad." Harvey remains

"Granddad" to friends today. Harvey felt as though he was a pretty good athlete. He liked swimming, but he also liked gymnastics. Harvey was inspired by his friend, Howard "Porky" Simmons. He admired Porky for his athleticism and agility and always viewed him with the highest regard. The reader will learn more about Howard "Porky" Simmons later.

In Harvey's first meet as a Shark, he placed fourth. He felt his breaststroke was his strongest, but he eventually moved to freestyle and, in college, swam the butterfly. Harvey had enrolled at Benedict College after high school and joined the swim team there. He practiced with the team from 7:00 a.m. to 8:30 a.m. each day. They generally competed against other HBCU swim teams, such as Johnson C. Smith University, Tuskegee University, and Alabama State University. Harvey noted that South Carolina State University was a very good team, but he felt Morehouse College was the most competitive and best team, in his opinion. Harvey remembers one meet in particular in which he was swimming the 400-meter butterfly. As there was no one from the other team entered in the race event, Harvey swam it alone to cheers from his teammates, "Come on, Granddad. Take one for the team." It was truly a badge of honor for Harvey to have the love and support of his teammates.

There have been several references made to being WSI certified by numerous other members of the Drew Park Sharks. As the reader is aware, several of the team's members were WSI-certified lifeguards. Unlike others, though, Harvey described in detail the process for obtaining his Water Safety Instructor certification. Harvey was certified, as others were, at Fort Jackson. Harvey notes he went to Ft. Jackson with another Shark for their certifications. There was a particular certification trainer at Ft. Jackson, a German-born man with the last name of Schmidt, and Harvey had the last class of the season. There was both a written and a physical component of the certification. Harvey recalls doing exceptionally well on the written component. There were 100 questions on the test, and one was required to score at least a 75 for a passing grade. The certification was complex. One was required to have knowledge of the rules in water safety, to know the nine strokes and the mechanics of each stroke, and to be competent in CPR; for water safety specifically, one must know about boating, safety equipment use, the cleaning of the pool, clean, safe water, PH levels, and filtering systems. Physically, one had to be competent in performing each of the swimming strokes, and you were observed above and below water for the correct style being performed. The certified individual had to have knowledge and be able to perform all life-saving techniques in retrieving a swimmer from the water. For WSI certification, one had to demonstrate basic to the most advanced rescue techniques to protect oneself when making a rescue. One had to demonstrate he/she had the endurance to perform rescues. One was required to know how to disable a swimmer who might be fighting for his life. The reader will recall how Chris Cochran described forcibly grabbing the man he was saving in the armpit to induce pain so the individual would focus on his pain rather than on his drowning, thus allowing the lifeguard to rescue him and bring him to the surface. Harvey said these were the techniques taught to perform a rescue to an individual fighting help. For a very large individual, Harvey shared that you were taught to lock your arms around the individual and to use the arm pit maneuver. In total, it was clear that obtaining your certification was a demanding exercise, and for the safety of individuals needing help, it was important to learn the lessons and knowledge.

With a degree in education from Benedict College, Harvey decided on graduate school at New York University. There, he majored in therapeutic recreation education. He was twenty-three years old. With his master's degree completed, he left New York City and moved upstate to work at the Rockland Psychiatric Hospital, where he spent three years. Following that experience, Harvey returned to Benedict College, and he taught for six years before obtaining his PhD at Bowling Green State University in Bowling Green, Ohio. With his PhD in hand, Harvey became the assistant dean of academic affairs at Benedict before moving to Winthrop College and later spending twenty-two years at the University of Central Michigan. Harvey and this writer have a mutual colleague who retired from Central Michigan. Harvey is currently employed at Wayne County Community College, where he serves as the vice chancellor for academic affairs.

Throughout Harvey's journey, as well as the journeys of each member of the Drew Park Sharks swim team, the reader has experienced the successes and positive experiences that have been a common theme. As Lindy Jeffcoat is fond of saying, the recipe for success is really quite simple—just add water.

REGINA BRANDYBURG CRUMP

Although far from the only female Shark, Regina Brandyburg was among the very first people to swim at Drew pool when it opened in 1950. Regina was a sprinter, and one news article reported that she won the 55-yard backstroke for Junior Women in eighty-one seconds. For non-swimmers, that is an amazing time for a woman in high school. The backstroke is one of the most difficult strokes, and the reader might recall that Lindy Jeffcoat referred to the backstroke as "controlled drowning." Regina was also a freestyle swimmer and a strong relay team competitor. At one meet in Jacksonville, Jimmie Ruff convinced Regina to participate in the diving competition, as they needed a female diver. She was required to perform a forward dive, a backward dive, and a flip. She said, "It wasn't pretty," but for the team, Regina was willing to do what it took, and she completed all three dives. Regina swam through elementary school and high school.

Regina recalls Drew Park still being named Seager's Park and praises the name change to Drew Park as a true day of celebration for the African American community. Born in 1944, Regina is one of the "early generation" swimmers to be a Shark. She lived and was raised near Benedict College on Laurel Street and Heidt Street and lived close enough to walk to the pool. Regina's mother and aunt were both swimmers, and it was her aunt, Clotelle Davis, who frequently accompanied Regina to the pool. Regina started swimming at the age of six. Clotelle worked as a librarian at Benedict College, and both of Regina's parents were high school science teachers. Her mother had degrees from South Carolina State University and Marshall College. Her father had degrees from South Carolina State University. The family often went on vacation to the beaches of the Carolinas and Florida, and everyone was comfortable in the water, so becoming a Shark seemed natural for Regina. She reports that Jimmie Ruff was one of her first coaches. The Sharks wore team jackets emblazoned with a shark, and when traveling to competitions in Jacksonville, Greenville, Greenwood, or other locations, Regina wore her jacket with pride, while other teams were envious of how the Sharks looked. To Regina, being a Shark meant so much more than just being a member of the team. It was being a member of the family or of the community that existed within Drew Park. It was a meaningful experience that she did not take for granted throughout her entire life.

After graduating from high school, Regina pursued her education at Michigan State University, majoring in education with minors in communication and classroom management. She later earned her master's degree in education from Western Connecticut State University. She taught in the Royal Oak area near Detroit, in St. Louis for six years, and in Westchester County, New York, until retirement. Regina shared that swimming was always a part of her life, as it is an outstanding form of exercise and a source of pleasure. The family had a pool in their backyard, and in Westchester County, she always planned an end-of-the-school-year pool party for her students and their parents. Regina also had a brother, Freddie, who swam and was a Shark. You will learn more about Freddie Brandyburg later.

Although Gigi, as her friends call her, talks about how good the other female swimmers were compared to her, she does so out of modesty. After all, Regina was an outstanding swimmer. One gets the idea that it's really her sense of camaraderie, support, and character that prevent her from promoting her outstanding skills. After all, Regina is a member of AKA Sorority, Inc., with its strong focus on sisterhood "by culture and by merit."

FREDDIE BRANDYBURG

s noted above, Freddie Brandyburg is Regina's younger brother. Born in 1947, Freddie, like his sister, was one of the early-generation Sharks. During our conversation, Freddie actually began where his sister left off. To Freddie, Drew Park, the pool, and the Sharks were connected and considered an extended family. He shared that he felt it was the older kids' responsibility to take care of the younger children who came to the pool and park, which was a distinguishing feature of life there. Older ones had watched out for him, and it was the tradition at Drew Park pool for each generation to care for and mentor the next. It was such a genuine feeling, and this writer could sense it in Freddie's expression as he shared the information. He left no doubt about his sincerity. Of course, at times, the younger kids were "little brats," getting themselves into trouble by running around the pool, not going through the showers to wash the dirt or sand from their feet, or simply jumping into the deep end of the pool when they couldn't swim. Freddie said that in his first year as a lifeguard, he rescued twenty-six people from the water. After the first year, he simply quit counting, though he and the other lifeguards routinely pulled people out of the water who had gotten into trouble. The reader will surely recall that Ellis Pearson, early in this collection of stories, said he jumped off the diving board and had to be rescued, and because of that experience, he taught himself to swim. It was Freddie Brandyburg who rescued Ellis on that eventful day. Freddie said it is very humbling when someone recognizes you as the person who saved their life or taught them to swim.

Although three years younger than Regina, Freddie indicated he was much more adventurous than his sister. Where she often walked to Drew with their aunt, Clotelle, Freddie ran ahead on his own, not waiting for the pair. He would head to Drew from their home on Laurel Street because he was so excited to get there. Like so many others, Freddie said his family loved Drew Park, and that sentiment has been echoed by just about anyone who ever swam or visited the park. Drew Park was their village.

Freddie shared how much he admired and respected the people in a leadership role at Drew pool. Like his sister, he too admired Jimmie Ruff. Freddie shared that each of his coaches worked to instill a high work ethic or standard in everyone who worked at the pool. "The coaches promoted a sense of pride and responsibility, whether we were in the pool, on the deck, or working in the basket room," noted Freddie. "They taught us how and when to be serious and focused. While we may not have known it at the time, we were being groomed for greater things, preparing us for life!" Freddie shared his admiration and respect for Jimmie Ruff. Freddie describes Jimmie as "more worldly" and more aware than many of his peers. To Freddie, Jimmie Ruff was a role model and "big brother" to him at the pool. He was more mature and "responsible" and served as a positive role model. Freddie learned from Jimmie how to balance the chemicals in the pool and operate the filter room. Today, thanks to Jimmie's lessons, Freddie balances the chemicals for his own pool. Freddie indicated he spoke with Jimmie on his cell phone, with the help of Jimmie's daughter, April, the day before Jimmie's death, during which he reminded Jimmie of all the positive memories they had shared.

Talmadge Dixon was another of Freddie's contemporaries. Though only one year older, Tam was a very good swimmer and pushed Freddie to improve. It is not unusual, when reviewing the archive photographs of swim meet results, to see that Freddie often placed directly behind Tam. Freddie acknowledged that his chances of winning an event improved when Tam didn't swim. While the two were competitors in the pool, they were good friends and enjoyed working together. Freddie shared that when Tam went to South Carolina State University, it was truly an eye-opening experience for him to see how much his teammates, who were mainly from the north, benefited from swimming and practicing year-round. Again, that reality has been further shared by Stanley McIntosh, who is a driving force behind Stanley's pursuit of outstanding facilities and coaching opportunities for the area's swimmers.

Freddie shared that his best stroke was the butterfly, and it was the stroke he liked swimming the most. He often swam the 50-meter and 100-meter events, and occasionally, the 200-meter events. In any competition, there were limits to the number of events one could swim, so that certainly played a factor in competitions. Freddie began swimming at the age of five or six, but he progressed quickly. It didn't take Freddie long before he was working in the basket room, around fourteen years of age, like so many before him. Soon after that, Freddie was sitting in the lifeguard chair. The reader has already read that one role of the lifeguard position was to assist with pool cleaning. You will recall the lifeguards "swept" the dirt, etc., from the shallow end of the pool into the deep end, where it would be vacuumed. Freddie shared that the lifeguards performed the vacuuming underwater. The lifeguards would don a mask and an air source like that used by scuba divers, but with no tank. The oxygen came from the air compressor on the deck. It was a significant addition to the understanding of cleaning the pool previously omitted.

After graduating high school in 1965, Freddie enrolled at Clemson University, where he was one of the earliest African

American students since its integration in 1963. Freddie majored in architecture for two years before switching to building construction. Freddie practiced with the school's swim team, where he was the only black participant. Many of the team's swimmers were from northern states where they swam year-round. He never participated in any competitions. Freddie completed his undergraduate degree in business administration and economics at Benedict College while simultaneously earning an associate degree in data processing and computer programming from Columbia Commercial College. He later earned a master's in public administration (MPA) from the University of South Carolina. His professional career included working at the South Carolina State Housing Finance Agency and the Department of Housing and Urban Development as an economist, conducting market studies and feasibility analyses.

Freddie shared a story that this writer had heard another individual mention in a conversation. He and the team were on a bus heading to a meet in Jacksonville, Florida, when the bus crashed into a car making an illegal turn. This writer is not totally aware, as of now, of the exact details of the injuries, but has been told there were several, and upon arriving at the first hospital, they were turned away due to the hospital not accepting Black patients. Freddie indicated he was not injured. Initially, local officials believed the bus had "fruit pickers" on it and not the Sharks swim team, according to Freddie.

TALMADGE DIXON

1946 - 2008

AS SHARED BY HIS WIFE, NARDA DIXON

Talmadge Dixon was born and raised in Columbia, South Carolina. Known affectionately as Tam to his friends, Talmadge's father died when he was three or four years old, and thus, he was raised by his mother. They lived in Saxon Homes, as so many other Sharks have noted. This is not the first time the reader has read about Talmadge Dixon. Gary Bell shares in his story about the relay race they won in a competition when Talmadge, swimming the fourth leg, destroyed his opponent. It is no stretch to believe Tam was one of the fastest sprinters, regardless of his stroke, the Sharks ever had on their team. This writer has seen no archived photograph of race results or archived news clipping in which Talmadge did not place first in his competitions. Race results demonstrate his prowess in backstroke, freestyle, and breaststroke across various age categories. Evidence is proof that Tam Dixon was an outstanding swimmer and team member.

Narda reports she first met Tam in high school at C.A. Johnson High School. Narda was not one to go to Drew pool as she grew up in rural Columbia though she was keenly aware that Talmadge did swim. She believed Tam maintained the football team's stats. After graduating from high school,

Talmadge attended South Carolina State University on a swimming scholarship. As a Drew Park pool lifeguard, Tam returned to the pool to work each summer. Tam was a sociology major. Narda attended Bennett College in Greensboro, North Carolina. Bennett College was an all-women's institution founded by the Methodist Church and recognized for excellence as an HBCU. She majored in special education and spent her entire thirty-five-year career working with special-needs children. She worked in Harford County, Maryland, Baltimore City, Maryland, and Martinsville, Virginia. Initially, Tam began work on his master's degree at Morgan State University, though he never completed it. He was employed by McCormick & Company, Inc., a spice company, in distribution. He later transferred to Miller Brewing Company in Eden, North Carolina, and remained there until his retirement. The reader will note that Tam is the first Drew Park Shark engaged in the business world as an employee of a business enterprise.

Narda fondly notes that Tam was very outgoing and friendly and always felt the companionship of his team members. He continued to swim throughout his lifetime and was a member of the YMCA in Virginia. It was said of Tam, "he never met an enemy." He was definitely a "people person" throughout his entire life. The couple had two children, and Tam taught each of them to swim. His daughter graduated from Morgan State University with a bachelor's and a master's degree and was a Fulbright Scholar. She spent a year in Trinidad, then obtained her PhD. She is a staff attorney for the New York City School System and resides in Brooklyn. His son attended Patrick & Henry Community College and Livingston College. Their son lives near his mom in Virginia and works for Allied Felts Manufacturing Company, specializing in CIPP Liners (cured-in-place-pipe).

What was most evident about Talmadge, as a Shark and a young, athletic male, was the confidence he shared with his teammates. As a role model, he demonstrated to his team that success was quite possible for each of them and not out of their control. They only had to believe in themselves that with hard work, they could achieve their goals. He thrived on the pressure of being the final swimmer in the relay race because they could sense his determination and grit would lead them to victory. If Tam had been given the opportunity, he would have been an Olympic competitor.

ROBERT "PLUTO" BRADLEY

A JOINT CONVERSATION WITH ROBERT AND HIS DAUGHTER, DAWN BRADLEY COOPER

"No worries." This was always Robert Bradley's signature phrase. Then again, if you were as fast a swimmer as Robert Bradley, it was probably a safe bet. Others only wished they could share his confidence. Gary Bell noted that he was a middle-distance swimmer but once had the idea of challenging Robert in a sprint. At a meet held at Johnson C. Smith University, Gary took him on in a shorter distance race. Gary indicated that after he was soundly beaten by Robert, he decided to stick with the middle-distance races.

In the 50-meter races, Robert was nearly unbeatable. This writer has seen the archived records. At a city meet at Drew pool, Robert ended the meet with the second-highest number of points. He was swimming in the junior men's category. The only individual to surpass his point total was James Evans, swimming in the senior men's category, and the total point difference between the two competitors was five points. The reader must remember that the junior men category was for boys aged fourteen to sixteen. Men seventeen or older were classified in the senior men category. There was no mention of the age gap between Robert and James. In another meet highlighted by the archives, Robert Bradley swam the 110-yard (100-meter) breaststroke, the 110-yard (100-meter) backstroke, the 55-yard (50-meter) butterfly, and the 55-yard (50-meter) freestyle and came in first place in each event that day. That's clearly a talented sprinter. Whether at Drew pool, university meets, or the Palmetto Games, one thing appeared certain about the outcome: Robert Bradley was taking home the trophies and ribbons for his outstanding efforts.

Born in 1942, Robert grew up on Reid Street in Saxon Homes. His mother was a nurse, and Robert's stepfather drove a cab. It wasn't until 1997 that Robert met his real father and his father's other family. His father had become a minister, and Robert had five siblings he had never met before connecting with his birth dad. This conversation was the first conducted jointly with Robert and his daughter, Dawn. Through the years, Dawn has reviewed past race results, been involved in numerous conversations with other Sharks, and has extensive knowledge of swimming, which places her in a valuable role to complement her father's life. This writer realizes he's written many words so far without mentioning that Robert was known to his friends as Pluto. You, the reader, had to know or be anticipating or expecting to learn Robert's nickname, as it seems every Shark had or still has one. Robert was known for staring out into space frequently as though he was searching for Pluto. Then again, he might just have been in deep thought about his life, his next competition, or his future. Knowing how bright his future was about to be, maybe he should have been named for the brightest star. Star might actually have been a more appropriate nickname, but it will remain Pluto.

Pluto was six years old when he began making the short trek to Drew pool. He offered to pick up trash, run errands for the lifeguards, or do anything he could to help them to get free entry to the pool or free swimming lessons. Given what we now know about the lifeguards, as reported by other Sharks regarding their behavior, it would be no surprise if Robert didn't get financial help from them. Like others before him,

Robert, too, became a lifeguard and water safety instructor at Drew pool. He played tennis in addition to swimming and later became not only a swimming coach but also the tennis coach at South Carolina State University. Robert holds the distinction of being one of the first African Americans to serve as a park ranger at Yellowstone National Park in Wyoming, as the reader learned about previously. Robert spent summers at Yellowstone National Park as part of the Department of the Interior summer opportunity for African American swimmers. A former resident of Saxon Homes, Robert was inducted into the Hendley Homes Wall of Fame for his service to the community. Robert earned a Bachelor of Science degree and a master's degree at South Carolina State University. He graduated from C.A. Johnson High School, where he lettered in football, basketball, track, and tennis. Bradley was inducted into the South Carolina State University Athletic Hall of Fame for coaching swimming and as a swimmer. After retiring from South Carolina State University, he taught health and physical education and served a term as interim athletic director for the Physical Education Department at Claflin University.

He and his wife Judy, also a nurse, had two children, Dawn and Rommel Holmes Bradley. Both children were born in Columbia and were competitive swimmers at a young age. They both also became lifeguards and water safety instructors, certified by their father. Later, both Dawn and Rommel served as lifeguards at Greenview Pool and taught swimming at the USC National Youth Sports Program (NYSP). It was interesting that his mother was a nurse, and he married a nurse. The family moved to Orangeburg in 1972 when Robert began working at South Carolina State University. Pluto had attended South Carolina State University, where he received his degrees. While in Orangeburg, Robert started a youth swim team called the Barracudas. The Barracudas competed across the state and region, even taking on the Drew Park Sharks. Dawn shared that she and her brother swam in any event that was needed to secure points for the team. She even swam in older age groups if it meant helping her team.

Robert and Judy divorced, and Judy moved to Boston with Rommel. Rommel worked at the City of Boston Community Center as a pool director. He also gave private swimming lessons. He now works for the City of San Jose in California. Rommel played tennis, football, and track in high school and earned his Bachelor of Science degree from East Tennessee State University. He was not only a scholar, but he also earned a scholarship to play football at East Tennessee State University. Dawn played volleyball and basketball in high school and received a basketball scholarship from the University of North Carolina at Chapel Hill, where she earned her Bachelor of Science degree. She went on to earn her master's degree from Emory University. She currently resides in Atlanta, Georgia, and writes grants and supports statewide college and career success initiatives for low-income students, youth in foster care, and other under-resourced students and families. Robert also had two additional sons from his second marriage. His oldest from his second marriage, Robert Jr., played tennis in high school and received an associate's degree from Denmark Technical College. His youngest son, Austin, played tennis, football, and baseball in high school and played football at Coastal Carolina University. He also earned a master's degree from Hampton University.

To Pluto, "excellence was a standard." It's been said that he was hard on his swimming team members, knowing that life would be hard for them later, and he wanted to do all he could to prepare them. He would often tell his swimmers, "Gentlemen, no matter what happens out there today, when it gets tough, reach into your back pocket, and you need to rise to the occasion." One of his swimmers shared, "I took it to heart and interpreted it as whatever it takes to be number one on that given day is the output needed to win the race."

HOWARD "PORKY" SIMMONS

The view from the lifeguard chair extends well beyond the sight of the pool waters. That's how Howard Simmons saw it. From that chair, watching the exceptional young swimmers, Howard could see into the future of the next generation of Drew Park Sharks and what he anticipated would be successful lives of the young men and women who swam each day at Drew pool. Like a young Ellis Pearson, Howard felt his eyes granted him the vision to see well beyond the current day. Howard lived in Allen-Benedict Court in one of the many apartments, so walking to Drew pool was a daily, short trek for him. He would arrive early and remain there all day. Howard shared that it was truly a good time and a positive experience for everyone. It was an amazing place to grow up and be with friends. Howard shared that the pool seemed to be located at the top of a hill of sorts, which seems to lend itself to a good metaphor for a "top of the hill" experience. Maybe Howard could see his future from that hilltop. Howard was actually playing Little League Baseball when he first became aware of the pool. His eyes and heart would become fixated on those pool waters.

Howard noted that Allen-Benedict Court was a series of apartment buildings with apartments lettered A to Z. There were twenty-six buildings, with nine to twelve apartments in each. He noted that Saxon Homes was a much larger complex, nearly surrounding Drew Park, and the pool was not far from C.A. Johnson High School. He recalls the baseball field being located on the site of the current Drew Recreational Center outdoor walking track. The indoor recreation building was a fun place to play marbles and other games. A not-unexpected fact: Howard had a nickname. In his case, it was one of his choosing. Not being assigned a nickname by others, Howard turned to one of his favorite TV shows, *The Little Rascals,* and chose Porky. Clearly, it was as good a nickname selection, and probably better than choosing Buckwheat, Alfalfa, or Spanky. Porky felt the name fit him well. One of his friends watched Porky eat a flower, petal by petal, on the TV series, so Porky was asked to do the same to prove he was deserving of the name. Of course, he ate the flower, petal by petal, and everyone seemed satisfied he was truly Porky.

Howard was eight or nine years old when he began swimming. He was born in 1951 and was a self-taught swimmer, similar to others the reader has met. Like many of his Shark peers, Howard became a lifeguard and worked each summer, even after graduating high school. Howard enrolled at Benedict College after graduating from high school. Howard said Harvey Dorrah was a good friend and a roommate during college, and that special bond was a signature feature of the Sharks. Following college, Porky and Domino shared an apartment. He had his heart set on a life in coaching. He majored in physical education only to learn later that few coaching opportunities were offered to physical education majors. It was almost a rule that schools didn't fill coaching positions from that major, which was disappointing to Howard, to say the least. Howard did find a passion and joy in his life, and this speaks strongly to his warm, caring personality. Howard loved working with the mentally challenged students, or exceptional students, as he referred to them.

His first job after Benedict College was with the State of South Carolina as a recreational therapist at an institution for individuals with mental disabilities. He was there for eleven years and fully implemented a physical education program for the participants. So, in a way, he was able to coach the students to complete exercises and physical activities for their benefit. One might say his service to that population was more essential and important than any high school athletic team. Fearing little to no upward mobility with that system, Howard enrolled at Midland Tech and received an associate degree in computer science and became a programmer. His salary increased, but from Howard's voice, this writer isn't sure his heart was as full as when working with the challenged students. He decided to become a real estate agent and obtained his real estate license. About the same time, Obamacare came along, and Howard worked as a "navigator" signing individuals up for healthcare. Howard's son was starting a business as a Medicare independent contractor. Howard, being a QMRP (qualified mentally retarded professional) with his educational and work experience, made him an ideal staff member for his son's company, and he transitioned to serving as his son's case manager. He remains employed with his son but found life returning to that first love of working with mentally challenged individuals, and he is so happy. He says that "he would do the work for free." We'll keep that point between us.

Something Howard definitely wanted shared with the readers is "his absolute relationship with my Lord and Savior Jesus the Christ of the only true living God, my wife of fifty years, and my twin sons." This writer is confident that Howard would want it shared that his wife's name is Barbara. She is originally from Ridgeway. Ryan and Bryan are the twin sons of Howard and Barbara, and Bryan's wife is Marian.

If the view from the lifeguard chair offered a fantastic vision, just imagine the view from the high dive. Howard shared that he enjoyed diving at Drew pool, though he readily admits that he was not as good a diver as Harvey Dorrah. In the conversation with Harvey, he failed to mention that he was a diver at Benedict College. It was his modesty that prevented him from bragging about his talent. Howard indicated he just couldn't get that twisting motion going, and he really only got to dive once in a meet. Howard said Harvey was a good friend and roommate in college, and that special bond was a signature feature of the Sharks. That bond was extended to another one of Howard's good friends, Domino Boulware. Howard and Domino became roommates following college. Howard loved swimming freestyle, but said, "Who didn't love that stroke?" Prior to COVID, Howard said he was swimming almost a mile each day at the Drew pool. After this conversation, Howard said he needed to get back in the pool. It's this writer's vision that leads him to make that commitment once again.

MARK HARKNESS

Mark Harkness's choice of words, as he shared his story, demonstrated he clearly had the ability to understand and share his feelings. In other words, Mark showed empathy as this writer had not seen in a while. Although the cost to enter the pool was twenty-five cents or fifty cents, for many during this period, that amounted to a considerable daily expense. I contemplated how individuals with so little could afford to visit the pool regularly. For his parents, both teachers and graduates of Allen University, Mark's mom was able to take advantage of the "summer discount package" by paying for the entire summer when she received her last paycheck of the school year. Mark's father, a principal, generally worked the summer, teaching summer school classes. Mark's father was also a realtor. Certainly, the readers are all aware that Sharks like Ellis Pearson mowed lawns for Saxon Homes residents, and we will recall that Pluto Bradley wanted to run errands for the lifeguards to assist with entry funds. Mark shared that he worked as a popcorn and peanuts vendor at the Carolina Coliseum to earn money. Mark clearly understood the burden that families endured to give their children such a wonderful opportunity. It could not have been easy growing up in public housing. These stories, though, have continued to shine a light on the sacrifices made to give the children such a fantastic opportunity. No one could argue that this community did not thrive on the love, friendships, teamwork, discipline, and respect shared by each member.

The reader will recall from his earlier story that Chris Cochran credited the Harkness family with his daily ride to the Drew pool. Their parents were friends, and both families lived in the Highland Park area. Chris praised and appreciated the ride with the four Harkness brothers. This is an interview that this writer looked forward to conducting. By far, this is the largest family of Sharks that might have existed at Drew. In nature, they'd be called various things, including a shiver, gam, herd, frenzy, or school. In real life, they were a family, joining the Drew Park Shark family. Their names are George, Tim, Mark, and Richard. Two sisters, Jennifer and Laurie, swam, but were not Sharks. George was the oldest and Richard the youngest. Mark was born in 1958. Like most other poolgoers, Mark said they generally arrived when the pool opened and stayed until 2:00 p.m. or 3:00 p.m. After securing a lifeguard position at the age of fifteen, remaining until dusk was not unusual. All four Harkness boys became lifeguards. George was five years older than Mark, and Tim was three years older. Richard was two years younger than Mark.

The reader has learned a great deal about the lifeguard position, including that lifeguards taught swimming lessons. Mark shared that, generally, the same two or three lifeguards taught the same individuals throughout their initial lessons. Generally, two lifeguards taught the intermediate classes, and the advanced swimming classes had their lifeguards in the deep end of the pool, where they also learned to dive. The lifeguards took pride in watching the individuals they taught develop. Every summer, there was a graduation, and each swimmer who had been taught participated in a swimming competition. The lifeguards loved cheering on the individuals they had taught to swim during the competition. It was just another reminder of the attention, care, and support that the lifeguards gave the young participants at Drew pool.

Mark shared that his favorite swimming events were the 110-yard (100-meter) freestyle and the 55-yard (50-meter) sprint. In reality, Mark was a strong swimmer and was very successful. He shared that, not since Lindy Jeffcoat, had there really been a faster swimmer at Drew pool. In addition to swimming, Mark was on the wrestling team, bowling team, and football team, and during high school, Mark served as a legislative page. Upon graduation from high school, Mark attended Johnson C. Smith University on a full swimming scholarship. In college, Mark swam the 500-yard, the 1650-yard, and the 200-yard freestyle, and the 400-yard individual medley. Mark majored in chemistry at Johnson C. Smith University. Tim and Richard, generally called Kip, also attended Johnson C. Smith University. Tim played football and swam, while Kip swam and played in the band. Tim received an academic scholarship and majored in business and computer science. The oldest brother, George, attended Clemson University and majored in building construction. Before graduating from high school, George was a track star and the South Carolina state champion in the 4x100-yard relay. The institutions they competed against while at Johnson C. Smith were very competitive, and many were very strong because they had large numbers of athletes from Florida and Georgia—in particular, Albany State University and, of course, South Carolina State University.

After graduating from Johnson C. Smith University, Mark accepted a job with Dow Chemical in Texas. He was there for six years. While in Texas, Mark lived near the space center, and, knowing Charles Bolden, he decided one day to visit him. Mark's wife had never met Charles. Mark relayed that he knew Charles' brother, Warren, much better, but he wanted to renew that Shark friendship.

In 1986, Mark went to work for Varian, a scientific instruments company. He moved to Atlanta in 1995 and remained with Varian. The company was purchased by another company in 2010, and Mark remained with the company until 2015, when he was laid off. He had begun pastoring in 2004 and, after being laid off, decided to pastor full-time. He continues to pastor in Atlanta to this current day.

Mark shared that he "owed everything to Drew Park." He repeated "everything" and shared, "It meant the world to me." The Drew Park pool was Mark's ticket out of Columbia, and it paid for his college education. He shared that Drew Park was a great place in the summer. "It was a sight to see on the fourth of July and Labor Day," he said. This has been repeated several times by various former Sharks. Mark said the cafe had the best hamburgers and hot dogs you could find anywhere. Mark stated that, while he was there and, as far as he could remember, in its history, Drew pool has no record of anyone drowning at the pool. That's a proud record of achievement over the decades the pool was in existence.

RICHARD "KIP" HARKNESS

Brother to Mark, George, and Tim, Kip rounded out the Harkness family swimmers at Drew pool. Kip is the youngest of the four boys. A friend of Chris Cochran and born the same year, 1960, Kip was taking swimming lessons by the age of eight. At nine, he was swimming competitively as a Shark in the Midget Boys category. Kip was a sprinter, focusing on the 50-, 100-, and 200-meter races. He recalled how good the swim team really was, as they competed against teams from Anderson, Hopkins, Greenview, and Orangeburg to name a few. As the pool at Drew Park was Olympic-size, Kip noted that many of his competitors struggled with the 50-meter length, since most of the other pools around were just 25-meters or even 25-yards. It clearly was an advantage for the Sharks to have trained and competed in the larger pool. For Kip, the breaststroke was his stroke of choice, though he liked swimming freestyle. He shared that he swam a little backstroke, but he drew the line at the butterfly. It would not be found in his repertoire. Kip proudly shared he held the pool record in the boys category (ages 11–13) for the 200-meter breaststroke.

At the age of fifteen, Kip was working in the basket room and became a lifeguard the following year. He worked every summer, even returning after his first year of college. Something this writer had not heard previously was that Kip reported the lifeguards gave adult swim lessons in the evenings at Drew pool. Certainly, many have shared their experiences teaching youth to swim, but this was a first for the writer, and Kip noted how much more difficult it was to teach adults to swim than it was to teach youth.

Kip attended WJ Keenan High School. The school band was known as the "Marching Keenan Raider Rubber Band." The school was named for William Joseph Keenan. Mr. Keenan was a business and financial leader and philanthropist in Columbia, and Kip noted that the students from the high school would periodically meet with Mr. Keenan for friendly conversations and to keep him abreast of school activities. During the academic year, Kip played football for four years, was a member of the track team for three years, joined the school wrestling team for one year, and played soccer. Keenan's soccer team was one of the first public high school soccer teams in South Carolina. Kip played on Keenan's first team. As a member of the Keenan High track team, Kip held the record for the mile run at 5:05. He also ran the 200, 800, and two-mile races.

Following high school graduation, Kip attended Johnson C. Smith University in Charlotte, North Carolina, on a swimming scholarship. Kip noted that following the implementation of Title IX, scholarships for the males were reduced to share the "wealth" with the women athletes, so after three years on the team, he accepted a college work-study position to help pay expenses. The reader will recall that Chris Cochran also attended Johnson C. Smith University, as well as Kip's brothers Mark and Tim. At Johnson C. Smith University, Kip initially majored in biology but changed his major to urban studies/community relations after his first year.

Upon graduation, Kip worked for the Columbia Urban League and sold shoes part-time. He later became a teaching assistant prior to enrolling in the seminary at IDC (Interdenominational Theological Center) in Atlanta, Georgia. He received his master's degree from Erskine Seminary School of Divinity and has been a pastor since 1983. He resides in Mount Pleasant, South Carolina, described as just across the bridge from Charleston.

Kip shared that Drew pool provided a great foundation for life. He stated that the older managers at the pool taught you to work smarter, not harder. There, he learned to "do everything well" and to appreciate the opportunities you received. He served as an assistant manager of the pool for three years and recalled teaching the staff at the Maxcy Gregg pool how to care for their water and keep it clean for swimming following a poor health check by the city. He coached swimming at Drew for a couple of years and recalled an annual meet at Fordham University. He noted the immense importance of providing young people with the opportunity for a safe, worthwhile, and purposeful activity, which swimming provided. It was an opportunity, as well, to provide "hope" for kids.

MONTEZ MARTIN, JR.

This writer isn't sure if the reader is aware that, in nature, sharks make a clicking sound. It was believed for some time that sharks could not make any noise and glided through the water soundlessly. Recently, though, it was discovered that sharks, though they have no vocal cords, make the sound by clicking their flat teeth together. Scientists believe the noise's purpose is either a stress response or a hunting strategy. The clicking can register to 156 decibels, which is equivalent to the noise a cap gun would make upon firing. The writer only shares this fact because Drew Park had a Shark who also made sounds with his drum. Montez Martin was a drummer in his high school marching band at C.A. Johnson High School. He also served as the band's drum major for three years. A snare drum has the maximum decibel level of 130. Montez was also a member of his high school newspaper staff and the yearbook committee.

Montez Martin lived his pre-teen years in the Pinehurst Community and later in the Waverly Community of Columbia. Born in 1940, Montez and Jimmie Ruff were class-mates and good friends. Small in frame, Montez recalls that as a sophomore and junior in high school, he was 5'4" tall. He liked swimming the 100-meter and 200-meter breast-stroke, his best stroke, though he readily states that Jimmie was much better and a much faster swimmer. Montez says he swam the 100- and 200-meter butterfly but seldom won competitions in those events. At Hampton University, Montez became a champion swimmer, setting Central Intercollegiate Athletic Association (CIAA) records in both the 100-meter and 200-meter breaststroke.

Montez began swimming as soon as the Drew pool opened. He lived close enough to walk to the pool each day. It was less than a mile walk. He credits the staff for how well and how efficiently they ran the pool. Montez says of the members of the staff, "They were instrumental in my life." He also noted, "It was just a wonderful experience," even if at times, he felt they weren't allowed to breathe. He also realized that there was a great deal of responsibility in managing the pool, and they needed to run a tight ship to ensure everyone's safety. It is interesting that the pool manager's grandfather and Montez's grandfather were brothers. As one of the earliest lifeguards at Drew pool, Montez shares that, again, the staff at Drew pool guided him through the lifeguard process, from obtaining his beginner's lifeguard permit to his senior lifeguard certification. Montez shared that later, Moses Hopkins conducted his senior lifeguard exam. With the support of the staff at Drew, Montez found a way to earn money to help pay his college tuition.

As a lifeguard, he was required to learn how the pool's filtration system worked. When Montez went to Hampton University, a position for a pool engineer was available. The position was advertised for adults and not for students. With his sister studying at Duquesne University, Montez needed the position because his parents were already struggling to pay her tuition. Montez met with the supervisor, who had little confidence that Montez could handle the job. He certainly felt a student could not handle the position nor have any idea of what they were doing. After being taken to the filtration room, Montez quickly discovered the Hampton pool had a fairly similar system to the Drew pool; it was just coded differently. Montez quickly figured out the system and began turning the required dials and valves. Upon being taken upstairs, he checked the pool's chemical levels. The supervisor was surprised and admitted Montez had been taught well at Drew pool. In addition, he was totally surprised to learn that Drew was a 50-meter, nine-lane pool for Black kids in Columbia, South Carolina. One summer, the Sharks had a competition in Greenwood, South Carolina, though Montez didn't swim that day. When the team returned, all they could talk about was the "bathtub" they used for competition that day. It was a little 25-yard pool, so it was clear to everyone what a fantastic facility they had at their disposal at Drew pool.

Speaking of parents, Montez's mom taught cosmetology at Booker T. Washington High School. The school had a trades department for high school seniors. She also operated Elise Beauty Salon and later Accent Wigs and Accessories from 1936 to 1987. Montez's father worked as a Pullman porter during World War II and afterward at Sears, Roebuck and Co. He later opened a linoleum and tile shop, Martin's Linoleum and Tile Shop, in 1949. In 1962, the shop closed, and Montez Sr. began working at Allen University, managing the maintenance and grounds. Later that year, he moved to Benedict College in the same role and retired from that position in 1977 at the age of sixty-five.

C.A. Johnson High School started a tennis team while Montez was there. He and several other students attended a tennis clinic at South Carolina State University taught by Victor "Vic" Seixas, an American champion who played in Australia and had previously won Grand Slam titles, including victories at Wimbledon and the U.S. Nationals. Vic instructed Montez and the other members of the team on backhand and forehand, as well as proper serving, among other aspects of the game. Montez indicated he was a much better doubles player than a singles player due to his size. It wasn't until well after college that he finally reached the height of 6'.

Montez graduated from Hampton University in 1963 and was commissioned as a Second Lieutenant into the Army Corps of Engineers. He spent seven years on active duty and served one year in Vietnam. He had also spent one year in Korea. He was in the Army reserves for twenty-one years. After returning from Vietnam, he was stationed at Fort Belvoir prior to becoming an ROTC instructor (assistant professor of military science) at the Polytechnic Institute of Brooklyn.

After leaving the active military, Montez worked in Atlanta, where he sold commercial time at WSB-TV. In 1973, he left Atlanta for Savannah, where he worked as station manager for WSOK am radio. In January 1974, Montez thought he would begin a migration to California, but he didn't make it out of Georgia. He landed a job at WCBD-TV in Charleston, South Carolina, as a news reporter. He felt the station was "looking for a Black face on TV," and they got one. After about eighteen months, Montez was employed by the College of Charleston as the director of construction until 1980. While working at the college, he earned his real estate license. Later, he obtained his real estate broker's license and opened his brokerage firm in 1976. The company was sold in 1994.

In his spare time, Montez was appointed to the Trident Technical College Board of Commissioners. He served on the board for nineteen years. Twice during that time, he was elected to serve as board chair. Later, the governor nominated him to serve on the South Carolina State Board for Technical and Comprehensive Education. Colloquially, the board is known as the Technical Education System. After selling the real estate company, Montez Real Estate, he was hired as the executive director of the Charleston County Housing and Redevelopment Authority.

Montez is the father of four children: Tanya M. Oube' Pekel, Terrie M. Rayburn (Wendell), Emily-Elise Martin, and Montez C. III. He said the lessons he learned at Drew pool were invaluable to him, whether he was fathering, leading the 536th Engineer Detachment (Port Construction) in Vietnam, or working as the assistant division engineer of the 2nd Infantry Division in Korea. The lesson that "people are people, and treating them with respect and dignity is all they want" helped him lead and excel long after Drew pool.

MILTON KIMPSON

With Milton Kimpson, there are so many recurring themes from the history of the Sharks that this writer could begin anywhere. Let's begin with the lessons learned from swimming every day with peers. Whether building relationships, riding in the car together to the pool each day, taking lessons from an early age through the various swimming levels every summer, or being part of a group of young Black kids going into the water together, Milton epitomizes all that is positive about Drew Park and the Drew Park pool. For Milton, swimming offered life lessons, positive relationships that have endured over the decades, discipline, determination, focus, work ethic, and confidence to take on challenges and succeed. From the outset, Milton states that he wasn't totally sure of his status as a full member of the Sharks swim team. He shares that his swimming talents leave much to be desired, though he adds that the backstroke is his favorite stroke. Why he selected the most difficult stroke as his favorite clearly speaks to his abilities. Milton shared that he did not compete often but recalls competing at the end of the summer in the Sharks' internal meet.

So, one must ask the question: If you work at learning to swim and can master a difficult stroke, isn't that experience worthy of being called a Shark? It's been reported earlier that not all Sharks became lifeguards and were water safety certified, but that alone doesn't rule out a person from being defined as a Shark. This writer played basketball in his freshman year of high school. Played is a word used generously, as he recalls maybe only getting into one game the entire season, and then only because the team was so far ahead that he could do no damage. But was he a Panther? Of course, he was a Panther. He met the criteria of being a team member playing for his high school, at least for that one year. Though basketball wasn't this writer's sport, he held two records in the high and low hurdles and shared a third as a member of the mile relay team. The writer was a Panther, just as Milton was a Shark. In high school, Milton played soccer at the YMCA. This is the first for this collection of stories. No one has previously indicated being on any soccer team. Milton also played the trumpet in the high school band.

Born in Columbia in 1961, Milton's family did not live far from Drew pool. Though he traveled to the pool most days with his friends, as one family or another took turns driving the kids, he said they sometimes walked from Lincoln Park. Lincoln Park was down Farrow Road, not more than a couple of miles from Harden Street. Milton shared that his parents recognized the importance of swimming and fully supported his efforts. He shares that his parents knew that if steered in the right direction, anyone could have a better life. Here again is that common denominator shared so often by Sharks. Milton has vivid recollections of passing through the various swimming stages, from beginner to advanced. Although comfortable swimming in the deep end of the pool, he was terrified of the diving board, and if allowed, he probably would have camped out at the end of the diving board rather than diving off it, as encouraged by Stanley McIntosh.

Milton's parents were both educators. His father, a graduate of Benedict College, was a principal at Carver Elementary. Milton recalls that sometimes, he would walk the three blocks to his dad's office after swimming lessons and ride home with him. Milton's mom was an elementary teacher and had a degree from Johnson C. Smith. Milton believes his parents' interest in his swimming was due to his mom knowing some members of the pool's leadership team. Milton said he grew up near Freddie Brandyburg's home and was aware of Freddie and Regina, though both were older than him.

After graduating from high school, Milton headed to Wofford College in Spartanburg, South Carolina. He knew at some point, his two siblings, who were six-and-a-half and eight years younger than him, would also have college plans. He knew they, too, would need financial help from his parents, so Milton accepted an ROTC scholarship to help pay for his education at Wofford. He graduated and was commissioned as a Second Lieutenant. He was granted an educational deferment by the Army to attend law school. Following three years in law school at Emory University, Milton was stationed at Fort Sill, Oklahoma, where he served for five years in the Judge Advocate General's Corps (JAG Corps), the military justice branch of the Army. At the end of his five years, Milton was transferred to Fort Jackson, where he continued his work as a judge advocate for two more years. Milton says he enjoyed his eight years in the Army and the reserves but decided to leave as he was required to spend too many weekends taking correspondence courses to remain a JAG officer. At the same time, Milton was engaged in his private practice and found both too time-consuming. He started with Johnson, Toal, and Battiste, a full-service integrated law firm where many young African Americans began their careers, either as interns or practicing. After working at smaller law firms, he learned that the South Carolina Department of Revenue needed litigation lawyers, so Milton accepted a position he held for thirteen years. In South Carolina, the State Legislature elects judges, and Milton decided to run for a seat at the South Carolina Administrative Law Court, where he served as an administrative law judge for seven years. Thereafter, he was elected to the South Carolina

Circuit Court and sworn in to fill an unexpired term in July 2024. If re-elected in February 2026, Milton will serve six years, beginning on July 1, 2026. Milton and his wife have two daughters.

Milton credits Drew Park pool and the management for instilling the drive to win. He said they learned that as young African Americans, they, too, "could do" stuff that would lead to success. Clearly, there's no better lesson that can be learned, and Milton and all the other Drew Park Sharks learned that lesson well.

EDWINA FIELDS

With swimming comrades such as Jimmie Ruff, Montez Martin, Virginia Brown, and both Brandyburgs, there could be no way to impede success. Thus, success is what Edwina Fields found at the Drew Park pool. Edwina moved to Columbia from Summerville, South Carolina, when she was eleven in 1951. The family lived near Farrow Road. It was perfect timing for the eleven-year- old Edwina, born in 1940, as the Drew Park pool was just opening. Edwina had girl friends who she said already knew how to swim when she began walking with them to Drew Park. They walked frequently until one reached the age of fourteen and could get a driver's license. She enrolled in swimming lessons and was a quick learner. Edwina said she wasn't sure that "Sharks" was the official name of the swim team early in its history. She recalls they were the Drew Park swim team.

For Edwina, the pool was something to do in the city and was considered the place to go in the afternoons. Edwina had the highest praise for each of the staff at Drew. That point has been obvious from just about every swimmer who passed through Drew Park. She shared that each one was so "valuable" to the city and the African American community. They knew how important it was and what it meant to the city. They expected a commitment, and as the reader is fully aware, they generally got what they wanted from the swimmers. To Edwina, it was simply a great opportunity to share with her friends, make lasting friendships, and develop skills, and she stated, "I loved it."

Something else Edwina loved was swimming the breast-stroke and the freestyle in competition, and she always felt comfortable swimming whichever leg she was given in a relay race. She was on the bus headed to the swim meet in Jacksonville, Florida, when it wrecked. As committed as the individual team members were, they still competed that day. They even performed their after-competition water show. She shared that one of the Sharks burned his foot diving through the ring of fire and let it hang out the window during the drive home. Edwina indicated her mother was on the bus as a chaperone. She said her mom often accompanied the team on trips. Edwina's mom stayed home early in her children's lives, but she later ran Wilkinson Homes, a Black orphanage in Lexington County, worked at the Bethlehem Center, and worked for the State of South Carolina at the girls' Reformatory on Broad River Road. She had a degree in home economics. Both of Edwina's parents graduated from South Carolina State University. Her dad was the principal at Waverly Elementary School, and he opened W.A. Perry School. He earned his master's degree from the University of Michigan.

Following high school, Edwina attended Talladega College in Alabama. She majored in biology and physical education. During her summers, she returned to the Drew pool to help teach smaller kids to swim. Edwina said she was not aware there were any female lifeguards during her time at Drew pool. She accepted a teaching job in Chicago after graduation, where she remained for four or five years. She returned to Columbia, attended the University of South Carolina, and received her master's degree. She remained in Columbia as a teacher for three years, but she did not like the situation stemming from integration. She planned to visit Occidental College in Los Angeles for one summer to support a friend, but she remained in Los Angeles for thirty-six years. She taught and later became an administrator in the Los Angeles School System.

As it has been predominantly covered in the recent news of today, Edwina shared she worked for USAID in Namibia, Africa. The U.S. Agency for International Development (USAID) is the principal U.S. agency for administering foreign aid and development assistance. Its primary purpose is to help countries experiencing conflict, poverty, or disaster, and to promote democracy and economic growth. USAID also works to advance U.S. interests abroad, including by supporting U.S. commercial interests and fostering goodwill. If that's not enough, Edwina worked for over ten years in Korea, visiting the country twice each year on a project with a friend. The reader is aware by this point that swimming can take you far. Few realize just how far it can take you.

WESLEY KENNEDY

The swimmers at Drew Park pool were skilled and talented beyond the general population, and most people were unaware of their capabilities. One day, with his father watching beyond the fencing around the pool, Wesley dove from the three-meter diving board. His father's immediate reaction was to scale the fence to come to his son's rescue. Even family members had no real awareness of just how proficient a swimmer their offspring really was. Wesley respected and admired his father, not just because he cared about his son's welfare in the water but because of the work ethic he demonstrated to his family. It was clear throughout our conversation that Wesley learned from his father, and with him as his role model, he would follow in his father's footsteps.

Wesley was born in Winnsboro, South Carolina, in 1948. Around the age of three, the family moved to Columbia and resided in Saxon Homes. Wesley shared that Saxon Homes had approximately sixty-four barrack-style buildings. They were solidly built homes and had several bedrooms in apartments, depending on the family's needs. The federally funded construction was bound by the railroad on one side and designed as a horseshoe, with Drew Park basically in the center. Wesley lived in building number sixty-three. As several other occupants of Saxon Homes have commented, it was an ideal location to walk to the pool each day, and Wesley shared, "It was a wonderful place to grow up."

Wesley began swimming at the Drew pool around the age of four or five, before moving into the Midget Boys group. He shared that he taught himself to swim and dive from a book he had found and read. He added that the young swimmers admired and looked up to the lifeguards, and as so many others have contributed, Foxy was one of the favorites. In addition to being good guys, most of the lifeguards were exceptional athletes who competed in a variety of sports. Wesley said he hustled for funds to get into the pool, collecting soda bottles for cash or whatever he could to earn the money to get in. Initially, he shared that the entry cost was nine cents, later increasing to eleven cents. Wesley added that though there was just so much to do at the park, it was easy to stay active and spend the day. The reader is aware of the many venues at the park, including the baseball field, sprinkler pad, community center, and a huge playground complete with a merry-go-round, a horseshoe pit, swings, and everything one could hope for. Most kids living at Saxon Homes got to be turned loose for the summer, and parents could not keep up with everything they were doing. It has been made quite clear, though, that the one thing they did not or could not do was get into trouble. The staff would have none of that, and everyone was well aware. It has been said in previous conversations that not only were the children who came to Drew Park known by the staff personally, but the staff also knew many of the parents, and the youth were well aware of that fact.

When Wesley was eleven or twelve, the family moved from Saxon Homes to a single-family home. It was a little outside the city, in a more rural area. It made it difficult to go to the pool as often, so there was a time when Wesley wasn't as involved in swimming. After a few years, Wesley was able to swim more, and at sixteen, he was trained as a lifeguard and water safety instructor. He recalls often scrubbing the "ring" around the pool with his lifeguard colleagues.

Wesley enjoyed swimming the breaststroke and felt he was good at it. He was also a good freestyle swimmer. Though certainly not his favorite strokes, he felt competent with his backstroke and his butterfly. Wesley said he had lots of red ribbons, of course, indicating second place. There were two meets in Columbia each year. Wesley gave a clear explanation of the difference between a "city meet" and a "state meet," which the Sharks competed in. The city meets were individual competitions, while the state meets were team competitions. In the city meets, members of the Sharks competed against each other as well as any individual who wanted to participate in the event and in the appropriate age category. In reviewing the race results from archived photographs, it's clear to see that someone from Columbia might take first place in a race while someone from Greenville might take second. At a state meet, the Sharks would compete against a team from Charleston, Greenwood, or Spartanburg, with points awarded to the team winning the event. Wesley indicated there were lots of really good swimmers at Drew Park. In both individual and team relay events, the Sharks were often the winners. Wesley recalls that one time he won a blue ribbon in the one-meter dive competition at a state meet.

Wesley described his father as a common laborer, though there seemed nothing "common" about him. There were times his father held three jobs. He possessed a great personality and a strong work ethic, and his employers recognized this through promotions in his various positions. His father worked as a janitor for the phone company, but, again, due to his personal traits, was promoted to the position of lineman and later to cable repairman, which he held until retirement. Wesley's mom did domestic work and was a seamstress.

Wesley offered great praise for his high school teachers. He said his teachers lived in the community and knew their students. He said they "cared about us." They offered discipline that might not have been pleasant at the time but was offered as a lesson in life and to help the individual for their lifetime. Wesley shared a statement the reader has already seen: He wished they could have gotten new textbooks occasionally, rather than always getting used books from the white schools. Wesley said they had a good mix of male and female teachers, which, in his opinion, was a good thing as males provided great role models. Wesley said with his teachers' guidance, you were taught you couldn't "coast into success."

After high school, Wesley was offered a swimming scholarship at Johnson C. Smith University, but with five younger siblings, he felt his family could not afford for him to accept it. He accepted a position with Southern Bell, which later became AT&T. He was drafted into the Army and served three years in communications, though he fortunately avoided Vietnam. Wesley took evening classes at Midlands Tech on the G.I. Bill after being discharged from the Army.

Wesley shared that being a Shark at Drew pool was simply "fun." The lifeguards had boxer-type swim shorts for when they were working, with red-and-white cross, lifeguard patches sewn on them. When team members raced, they wore Speedos, tight-fitting brief-type swim shorts, that had the patch sewn on them. Wesley stated that he was proud to wear the red-and-white lifeguard patch on his swim shorts.

CAROLYN FAIR

JUDY FAIR (1947 – 2015)

AS SHARED BY HER SISTER, CAROLYN

There were two Fair daughters, but if one was not aware of the family, most would have thought the family was much larger. If Carolyn and Judy were together, it was a pretty safe bet that at least one other neighborhood friend was with them, and generally more. Carolyn was the oldest, born in 1944, with Judy three years younger. Someone would generally drive the two young girls and any neighborhood friends to the pool each day, but occasionally they would sneak away and walk to the pool from their home on Laurel Street. The reader is aware that Laurel Street is near Benedict College. Carolyn shared that it was a sure bet they were at the pool every day, which is a statement repeated numerous times throughout this work. Carolyn also set the record straight about female lifeguards. The girls were lifeguard certified, having successfully completed the lifeguard course. The pool's manager wanted them to know how to rescue someone, though no females were actually hired. There was a belief that girls might have difficulty safely getting a larger person out of the water, so no positions were held by females.

Carolyn and Judy's parents were both educators. Their father taught history and served as a coach for Lakeview High

School, while their mother taught third grade for the Richland District 1 School. Their mother frequently taught summer school. With mom at work during the summer, the girls convinced their father to build them a lemonade stand. The girls sold lemonade in the Benedict College neighborhood to earn money to pay for the pool's entry fee. Once she learned of its existence, their mother did not approve of the lemonade stand. Dad and the girls had hidden the idea from their mother, well aware of her feelings about it. One thing in particular her mom did not favor was the girls getting their hair wet each day. Others have told this writer that this is one reason so few Black women enjoy swimming, or that it prevents them from learning to swim. One person noted that if you fall off a ship or out of a boat or anywhere in deep water, probably the last thing you're worrying about is your hair.

Both girls were outstanding swimmers, and each swam throughout the summers in age- appropriate categories. One only has to review the swimming results posted in the newspaper archives to regularly see both Judy and Carolyn's names winning individual events and relays. Like every Drew Park Shark, the girls could swim any stroke, though each had a favorite and "go-to" stroke. For Carolyn, it was the breaststroke, and for Judy, it was freestyle events in most competitions.

Both Carolyn and Judy were involved in various clubs throughout high school and swam each summer. After graduating from high school, Carolyn enrolled at Fisk University in Nashville, Tennessee, where she majored in biology. She moved to Washington, D.C., attended Howard University for a master's degree, and later earned her PhD in science education from the University of South Carolina. Judy also earned a PhD in social work from the University of South Carolina, after earning her bachelor's degree from Fisk University and her master's degree from Atlanta University. Judy worked as a social worker for the Urban League in Atlanta and for

Atlanta Public Schools. Upon returning to Columbia for her doctoral work, Judy was employed by the Department of Social Services and the Richland 1 school District. She was very active in local associations prior to her untimely death in 2015.

Carolyn taught elementary, middle school, and high school for approximately four years while living in Washington and attending Howard University. She returned to Nashville to teach and serve as a Coordinator at Fisk University, where she remained for four years. She left Nashville and lived and worked in Mississippi, where she taught at Sacred Heart Academy in Ocean Springs. Carolyn returned to Columbia and taught at Brooklyn Casey High School and Lexington District II. She accepted a position at the Governor's School for Science and Mathematics, where she served as the vice president for outreach. The school was a residential school, with every student receiving a scholarship. Her focus in the position was to assist students in developing research projects and to provide summer opportunities for middle and high school students. During her career, Carolyn served as the associate director of South Carolina Education and as president of the National Science Teachers Association.

Returning to our conversation about Drew Park, Carolyn shared that her first job was as a basket girl. None of the males to date have referred to working as basket boys. Each has indicated they worked in the basket room. Carolyn indicated that Judy also worked with Charles Bolden Jr. in the basket room. The readers will remember that the Fair family managed the snack bar. Carolyn shared that they only did that a couple of summers, and swimmers could carry an account at the snack bar until the week's payday when they cleared their account. Carolyn noted that there was strong support to succeed at Drew Park, and at times, they were even "pushed" to succeed. This time, the reader hears from Carolyn that the Drew Park pool made for lasting relationships. One worked and swam with individuals who later were your co-workers in other jobs, peers in organizations, sorority sisters and fraternity brothers, and friends throughout your life.

RONALD ANDERSON

"Scum, gutter, flutter," probably not how one would anticipate any story beginning, but to this writer, it was so unusually humorous that he couldn't resist. What is it? It's a name made up by Ronald and the two McIntosh boys, Stanley and Stephen, and it had to do with their early morning routine of getting the pool ready for the morning's opening. Each morning as they entered the pool area, they had to get into the chilly water and begin scrubbing the "ring" around the pool from the previous day. The three senior lifeguards made it into a competition, and the winner got the first break as opposed to having to occupy the lifeguard chairs. If the reader recalls, there were three lifeguard chairs, and throughout the week, two were occupied at one time. The third individual, though on break, still monitored the pool deck. On busy weekend days, all three chairs were occupied. Anyway, two of the three boys would begin scrubbing in the deep end, which required one to "flutter" or stay afloat while holding a brush and a one-gallon bucket of soap. The fluttering motion was with your legs moving to keep you above water. The gutters were around the deck to direct water outflow and keep trash out of the pool. Whichever lifeguard made it to the shallow end while cleaning first got the first break the following morning, thus two were competing each morning.

Ronald indicated there were other ways the lifeguards competed against each other as well. There was a chart in the office for capturing the number of rescues each lifeguard made. Whenever a rescue occurred, the lifeguard who made the rescue was awarded a gold star, which was placed next to his name on the office chart. As the reader may recall, Freddie Brandyburg commented that he made twenty-six rescues in his first year, one of them being Ellis Pearson. This writer didn't ask at the time how he remembered, but it has now become clearer. Ronald shared that it wasn't unusual for more than one lifeguard to attempt any rescue needed. Each wanted the gold star. Not really, for each lifeguard was so committed to keeping the swimmers safe, each would rush to save someone in need. The "star" was just a nice recognition.

Born in 1955, Ronald has a twin brother, Donald, who also swam at Drew pool as a Shark, though Donald was not a lifeguard. They have a sister, Gail, who also swam on the team. She was two years younger than Ronald and Donald. In all, there were ten Anderson children, six girls and four boys. Ronald and Donald were number eight and nine. Their mother wanted them to learn to swim, and though several were born before the pool was built, Ronald said all the kids swam at Drew at some point. Born in Columbia, the family lived in several different homes, with none very far from Drew Park. All the homes were relatively near each other. They lived off Farrow Road and Colonial Drive in a community called Colonial Heights. Ronald and Lindy Jeffcoat were good friends and lived relatively close to each other. The only thing the moves affected was the schools Ronald attended, as some homes were zoned to a particular elementary or junior high school. Ronald's house was in an area that required him to attend Columbia High School. He attended Sara Nance Elementary School and Withers Elementary, based on the house he was living in at the time, and Alcorn Junior High School. As mentioned, he was zoned to attend Columbia High School, but being small in frame, Ronald indicated he wasn't prepared to attend high school with white people. He had been bullied by Black peers, but being bullied by white kids was something he could not tolerate. He informed his mom that, following the first week of school, he wanted to leave Columbia High School. Ronald's grandparents lived nearby, and he used their home address to attend C.A. Johnson High School.

Ronald began swimming at Drew pool at an early age. "When you arrived at the pool, you could hear everyone," stated Ronald. He shared, like so many others, that Drew pool was his summer babysitter. It was a "safe environment" and "you were never alone" were additional comments. Ronald said, "Drew pool watched out for you," and, "It was part of your fabric." Ronald said Drew pool was his "first exposure to real trust." Ronald shared that he had a number of close friends at Drew pool. Most of his memories of his time at the pool come from conversations with his friends. Ronald indicated he grew up in a disciplined family. We were taught to listen and observe rather than speak. Ronald was left-handed, so he seemed to gravitate toward left- handed friends. He had a friend who was the quarterback of his high school football team, and the two of them talked about life every day. None of the members of Ronald's family were permitted to play any contact sport, so swimming was ideal for Ronald. His natural stroke was the breaststroke, and he was exceptional. That defining word came from other Sharks within these communications. Ronald noted Lindy (or Ben) was a freestyle swimmer, and Ellis (Ray) Pearson was a butterfly guy. He noted the Harkness brothers were tall, which made them good at the backstroke. To get acclimated to the pool each day, Ronald said they swam the length of the pool underwater.

Ronald became a lifeguard at fifteen and worked for three years. He was also a senior lifeguard. He was a crew chief and WSI-certified. His role, in part, was to determine which chair you began in for the day, as well as to handle other responsibilities, and the position earned slightly more per hour. The lifeguards learned how to enter the water for a rescue. One would either shallow dive under the person and use their momentum to bring them up or enter feet-first and let the splash push them toward the wall. They learned to enter the water with finesse, sometimes diving from the lifeguard chair.

In high school, Ronald ran on the track team and tried out for the basketball team, but admits he wasn't very good. He was in the high school choir, certainly a non-contact activity. After high school, Ronald went to Talladega College in Alabama. Ronald only remained at Talladega College for one year. He had always heard that if you ever got into trouble with the "law" in Alabama, you'd probably never leave Alabama, so after being "tailed" one day, he made the decision to leave. While at Talladega College, though, Ronald received a work-study position to operate the campus pool. Unfortunately, the campus gave Ronald no budget for chemicals, no pool lighting, and no cleaning materials. Clearly, it was virtually impossible to maintain the pool in those conditions. Ronald returned to Columbia, but with advice from his brother, Donald, who was serving in Korea at the time, Ronald asked his mom for $1,000 and, in return, promised her he would get on the "right track."

Ronald decided to attend Clark University in Atlanta, where he majored in education. While there, he audited a class in military science, and though he thought he wasn't interested in the military, he said he found his new calling and the structure he had so desired for his life. Ronald received a great deal of support from a Black major, which helped him overcome some issues he encountered from a white Colonel, who hampered his scholarship. He graduated and received a highly coveted position in the medical service corps as an officer.

While in Atlanta attending college, each military student from all the local universities came together for one class at the Georgia Institute of Technology. At a ceremony at Georgia Tech, Ronald was awarded a medal of "zero significance" entitled Medal from the Sisters/Daughters of the Confederate Union.

Later, as a platoon leader in the tank battalion, Ronald managed the battalion's medical aid station. Ronald indicated he always tried to change things that needed to be changed for the benefit of everyone and always attempted to speak up for the "least and left behind." Ronald retired from the military as a major. He later worked as a Department of Defense contractor and a Defense Department program manager, focused on military healthcare. He retired at age sixty-two. He and his wife, Brenda, have a blended family with four children.

DR. VIRGINIA BROWN LOCKHART

Virginia Brown's life could easily be characterized by her "firsts." She was one of the *first* individuals to swim at Drew pool when it opened in 1950. As a ten-year-old girl in 1950, she was among the *first* to take swimming lessons, taught by her brother John A. Brown, who was hired as one of the first lifeguards when the pool opened. John had served in the Navy, where he became a proficient swimmer; thus, he was hired as one of the *first* lifeguards at Drew. John was nearly eighteen years older than Virginia. She was one of the *first* women to learn how to balance the pool at Drew Park. Taught by her brother, she was later able to balance the pool at her family's home in Los Altos Hills, California, when she lived there. Virginia learned to swim rapidly, and competitors frequently watched from behind her as she touched the wall in *first* place. Virginia was fiercely competitive and was unmatched in the 50-meter freestyle. Her time in the 50 equaled that of the world record at that time. The current world record for the 50-meter freestyle is held by Jordan Crooks of the Cayman Islands at 20.08 seconds. Virginia was the *first* to defeat a male swimmer from Morehouse College, considered to be their best swimmer. He was, by the way, the brother of Aretha Franklin. Virginia is the *first* female Shark to admit she had a nickname: Squirt. Although Virginia was not the first Shark arrested for civil disobedience at the time, she was the *first* to be arrested alongside Dr. Martin Luther King, Jr. and accompanied him to jail. She spent fifteen days in the

Fulton County jail. However, Virginia was the *first* Shark arrested twice for civil disobedience. The second occasion brought her face-to-face with the infamous Bull Connor when her bus was stopped in Anniston, Alabama, and she was sent to jail once again. Clearly, she was a *first*-class member of the Sharks, and what she calls the community development opportunity of a lifetime: to be part of the Drew Park family.

Growing up in Columbia, Virginia lived on Haskell Avenue, so she could walk to the pool each day with her sister, Delores, who was two years younger. Her father was the dean of theology at Benedict College and the pastor of the Second Calvary Baptist Church. The parsonage they lived in is currently the International House for Visiting Professors at Benedict College. Her mother was a housewife. Virginia shared that her father, a leader among the area's NAACP, did everything possible to shield her and her sister from the effects of the Jim Crow laws, including never having them use the segregated bathrooms or drinking fountains when traveling, or never riding a bus, where they would be required to sit in the back.

Virginia shared that Drew pool was so impactful to her life, and there were so many lessons learned from teamwork, mutual respect, diligence, and working hard for your accomplishments. She recalled the constant swimming back and forth at the pool during practice, building endurance, learning every stroke, and becoming not only stronger but also faster. Virginia was a 50-meter sprinter. Her sister Delores was always there next to her, and Virginia shared that Delores was her strongest competitor and actually broke one of the records set at the pool by Virginia. Virginia enjoyed diving, though she never dove competitively. She was a strong breaststroke and backstroke swimmer but readily admits that her weakest stroke was the butterfly. Like the other female swimmers at Drew, Virginia learned to be a lifeguard. She utilized that knowledge later in college, where she served as a lifeguard and taught the faculty's children to swim.

Virginia's father passed away when she was seventeen, so she needed a job in college to help pay expenses. She swam through high school, and at the age of seventeen, graduated and enrolled at Spellman College. She recalled her grandmother had also attended Spellman College. Prior to high school graduation, Virginia said she was inspired in school by her ninth-grade science teacher. It was her teacher, Charles Bolden, who led Virginia to a life devoted to science. Virginia shared that Mr. Bolden helped her dad find her first microscope and her first chemistry set. At Spellman College, she double majored in psychology and biology, with a minor in education.

Following college, Virginia moved to Sacramento, California. She became a clinical lab scientist with her interest in biology and, while there, met her future husband, who was doing his medical school residency. She worked at that position for twelve years before heading back to school for a master's degree in clinical psychology at San Jose State University. Virginia then pursued a Doctor of Education degree in educational administration from Nova University. Nova offered classes at the University of California, Berkeley. Virginia remained in Silicon Valley working for both Varian Associates (MRI machines) and Hewlett-Packard, where she traveled the world training managers, and from where she retired. Her husband set up a private practice in Menlo Park, where the couple lived for thirty-two years. Upon retirement, they moved to San Jose.

Virginia shared she had such fond memories of swimming at Drew Park. She loved the women's swimsuits they wore and talked about her swimmate, Charles Bolden, Jr. and how tough the staff was in the management of the Drew pool. All this together offered her comfort, as she truly belonged to a family at Drew. She was saddened to hear about how the original pool had been demolished and replaced with one less than half the size. For Virginia, Drew Park meant everything for the African American community and for her personally. She continues to treasure the relationships developed there.

DELORES BROWN

The reader is already familiar with Delores Brown from her being mentioned throughout her sister's history. Having more than one family member who swam competitively is fairly typical. Delores Brown, though, was anything but typical when it came to swimming. She was one of the faster members of the swim team, and her sister, Virginia, could attest to that fact. Virginia had to work hard because of the constant challenges from Delores. That competition made both women stronger, and for the team, two winning members.

Delores was soundly reassuring during the conversation that the Drew pool was "my pool." That feeling of ownership has been pretty much a consensus throughout each shared history, but Delores was flatly stating what others may not have said so explicitly. To each individual who visited, swam, or played in the water, Drew Park pool was a very personal experience. Delores was also very proud that the pool offered her a job throughout high school. She worked daily at the entry gate, selling and collecting entry tickets. It was her first work experience and one that was not only fulfilling but also meaningful to her. That work ethic became a trademark of sorts for Delores, as the reader will learn. The reader is already aware that she was taught to swim by her older brother, John. His swimming lessons for Delores and Virginia actually began long before Drew pool. John taught the entire family to swim in the ocean during family vacations to Atlantic Beach. Atlantic

Beach was the segregated beach for African Americans during this time, since Blacks were not permitted to swim at Myrtle Beach and Hilton Head Island.

As a Shark, Delores competed in the freestyle, backstroke, and breaststroke events. Virginia indicated Delores was often her stiffest competition, and you will recall that Delores broke one of her sister's records at Drew. The two sisters were very strong swimmers in the sprint events and generally disposed of any competitors with ease. They practiced together every day, making each other stronger and faster swimmers.

Delores was in the living room watching TV when she called for her parents to come and see the news. There on the television set, they watched as Virginia was being arrested along with Dr. Martin Luther King and being hauled off to jail. This writer is sure that made for some interesting family conversation. Virginia previously mentioned that her father was the pastor of 2nd Calvary Baptist Church, but Delores shared that her father, the Reverend Charles Henry Brown, was also extremely well-versed in the ancient Semitic languages of Hebrew, Greek, and Aramaic. He frequently translated old documents and used them in his theology classes at Benedict College.

Delores attended American River Junior College in California for her first two years, then transferred to Benedict College to complete her academic work. Following graduation, she worked at the UC Davis Medical Lab. The lab at the time had a grant focused on sickle cell anemia. Sickle cell disease is a disorder that causes red blood cells to become misshapen and break down, leaving a shortage of healthy red blood cells. Delores later served as a lab technician at the UC Davis Medical School, specializing in blood banking. She supervised the education program for clinical lab technology. She earned her master's degree as well.

KAREN BROWN

On this golden anniversary of the film classic *Jaws,* petite, shy, and even demure Karen Brown had her competitors in the 50-meter breaststroke and the 50-meter backstroke echoing the movie's famous line, "We're going to need a bigger boat." Her competition could simply not fathom how such a small, young girl could have such a competitive drive. Of course, Karen begins by stating she could not have been so successful without her mother's "magic drink," which she was given each morning on competition days. The drink was stimulating and boosted her confidence, even though it was just grape juice and honey. Upon hearing the sound of the starting gun, she swam her heart out, never looking back at her competition until she touched the wall.

The daughter of John Brown and niece of Virginia and Delores Brown, it appeared the apple did not fall far from the tree. Born in 1957, Karen learned to swim like her relatives in the ocean and in the pool from her father, John. "Drew was life," according to Karen, and both racing and practice were "exhilarating." It was a "community of happiness." Swimming afforded me confidence in myself. I had the feeling I could accomplish anything, and if someone else could do something, so could I. Practicing and competing offered lessons in drive and ambition. All of these were Karen's feelings about being a Shark.

Karen lived on Frye Road before her father accepted a teaching job in California. Since the age of four, Karen had lived at the Drew Park pool, and moving was nearly catastrophic for her. She had learned to swim at Drew, first learning to hold her breath underwater, to float in the prone position, to kick and move her arms properly in the water, and to turn her head to breathe. What seemed to be simple tasks provided Karen with the technique, physical attributes, and strategy to be successful. She carried those traits throughout life. Upon moving to California, Karen had no pool access as a middle school student but was able to resume her competitive swimming during high school, where she displayed the same winning skills she had demonstrated as a Shark.

In California, she began at a junior college, which offered the first two years for free. Following that, she attended De Anza College for two years. Following junior college at De Anza, she pursued full-time employment at Memorex for several years. She also held a position with the Oakland Thoracic Health Science, helping people with lung diseases. At twenty-two, Karen began college again at San Jose State University, where she earned her bachelor's degree in 1985 as a health science major. She met her future husband there, and two years later, they were married.

Karen held several positions after graduating from San Jose State University. In addition, she earned her K-6 teaching credentials. She held a part-time job as a health clerk for the school districts from 1999 to 2004, when she earned her own classroom. She worked with students transitioning from a foreign language to English in a program called EL (English Learners), where she assessed their progress in reading and writing in preparation for entering the classroom. Karen retired in 2017. She and her husband have three children.

HENRY KENNEDY

As the first cousin to Gary and Thaddeus Bell, Henry Kennedy shared, like many before him, he virtually lived at the Drew pool from sun-up to sundown each day. Henry started swimming at around age five and was actively learning to swim almost immediately. He stated he had fond memories of the people there and the "family environment" created at Drew Park. One particular family he enjoyed was that of our friends, Rick and Carl Thomas. Henry indicated he had never known Carl to be called anything but "Hightower" because of his fantastic diving from the high board. Carl, it appears, was one of those individuals with multiple nicknames, so it's possible, after all these years, that one cannot be entirely sure which family he was referring to. He was "an outstanding diver, handsome, and great to watch," declared Henry.

His memories of Rick were just as equal, as he recalled how fast and how smoothly Rick moved through the water. Henry shared that Rick had longer hair, which he often shook when leaving the water, and he tried his best to imitate that head shake, though his hair was cut short by his cousin's dad, the barber. "It was a special time," Henry said, and "a great recreational outlet for the Black community at large."

For Henry, though, most of his competitive swimming occurred not at Drew pool. At the age of nine, Henry's family moved to Washington, D.C. Henry had been born in Columbia in 1948, and initially, his family lived with his maternal grandmother at 1010 Oak Street. The family later built a home in the Columbia suburbs. Henry shared he spent a great deal of time with his cousins at their initial home in Allen-Benedict Court, within walking distance to the pool. In Washington, D.C., the family lived in a couple of different locations, and Henry shared that to go to swim practice each day at the YMCA, he would catch a bus for an hour ride, practice, and then head to school to be on time. The YMCA where Henry swam was near the White House. Henry was the only Black member of the Y team and was selected as its captain.

Henry indicated he was an outstanding swimmer, and at the age of eleven in Washington, D.C., he was offered the opportunity to practice with the Howard University swim team each day. He got to travel to meets with the Howard University team occasionally and often warmed up with them. Henry credits his dad for meeting with the coach of the Howard University team, Dr. Clarence Pendleton, to get permission for his participation. Of course, he could not compete, but just imagine getting the opportunity to practice with a university team at that age. Henry could swim all four strokes, but his favorite stroke was the breaststroke.

Henry shared a fascinating story about his father. His father's mom died within twenty-four hours of his birth. His mother's grandfather was white, and he married a Black woman. Henry said his grandmother's mother was a slave and the mistress of a white slaveowner who, upon his death, left her property, which became the family farm. They grew sugarcane on the farm. Henry's mother's sisters took him in after his mom's death, and his dad grew up on the farm in Louisiana. Later, Henry's grandfather remarried and took Henry's dad to New Orleans to live.

Henry's dad always wanted a family. Maybe it was because of his unique upbringing, but a family meant a great deal to him. Henry's mother was sixteen when she married his father.

They kept the news from everyone at the time. Henry's dad had joined the Army, and they met at the USO. They were married within three weeks of meeting. Henry's mom had been admitted to South Carolina State University, but at the time, married women were not accepted, so she kept her marriage secret and completed her degree in education. His dad had been transferred to a base in Kansas from Fort Jackson, and upon a visit, a local cab driver recognized his mom and refused to take the couple to a local motel. The couple was forced to reveal the marriage to her family. Henry's mom wanted an advanced degree, but colleges and universities in South Carolina would not permit Black women to take advanced degrees and actually paid them to go out of state. Henry's mom attended New York University, and he stayed with his cousins, the Bells, while she was there.

Henry shared that his father always seemed unrealistic and unforgiving. While living in Washington, D.C., Henry competed in an AAU swim competition in Northern Virginia. The times registered in the competition were to be used for the Olympic trials. Henry didn't do well, coming in next to last. His unforgiving dad told Henry he needed a new sport. That year, for Christmas, he asked for a ping pong table, but on Christmas morning, Henry found a tennis racquet and a can of tennis balls instead. Henry immediately went outdoors, found a wall, and began hitting balls against the wall. He quickly learned he really enjoyed tennis. Henry played tennis in high school.

Henry graduated from high school and attended Princeton University. He played tennis at Princeton. He majored in history, sociology, and economics. He was in the Woodrow Wilson School of Public and International Affairs. Upon graduation from Princeton, Henry attended Harvard University School of Law.

Following law school, Henry accepted a job at the law firm Jones, Day, Reavis, and Pogue. After that, he joined the Assistant U.S. Attorney's Office for the District of Columbia, a position he held for three years. He was appointed as a U.S. Magistrate, the youngest person ever appointed by the judges of the U.S. District Court. The United States Magistrate is a judicial officer in the federal court system who assists U.S. District Court judges. He held that position for three years. President Jimmy Carter appointed Henry to the Superior Court of the District of Columbia, and he remained in that role for eighteen years. The Superior Court of the District of Columbia was established by Congress as the trial court of general jurisdiction for the District of Columbia, prosecuting most non-federal crimes committed in the District of Columbia. President Bill Clinton appointed Henry to the U.S. Federal District Court, where he served for fourteen years before his retirement.

Henry has continued playing tennis and swimming. He is a seven-time National Black Champion of the American Tennis Association. He won championships in the following age group divisions: 35, 45, 55, and 65.

Henry has two siblings, a brother, Randall, and a sister, Angela. Randall is a respected legal scholar on race in the U.S. He is a graduate of Princeton and Yale Law School, was a Rhodes Scholar, and a clerk for a Court of Appeals judge. He served as Thurgood Marshall's clerk. Randall is the youngest tenured faculty member of Harvard Law School, a professor of law, and the author of four books. Angela is also a graduate of Princeton and Howard Law School and serves as a public defender in Washington, D.C. Angela and Michelle Obama were Princeton roommates and are best friends.

Henry has two daughters, Morgan and Alexandra. Both are Princeton graduates as well. Morgan played the flute in the orchestra, graduated Magna Cum Laude, won an award for the best thesis in Harvard Law, and currently represents Google.

After graduating, Alexandra went to work for Under Armour and later became its chief of staff. She later worked for Twitter before becoming executive vice president of My Code.

Henry says he is a man of strong opinions and beliefs. Then again, Henry was at Drew Park swimming under the tutelage of wonderful staff members with very strong beliefs about life, behavior, determination, and commitment. Henry defines success as a person who develops and maintains good character traits such as honesty and kindness. Without doubt, the Drew Park pool staff at all levels had these traits instilled in them and drilled into them from the time they first entered the grounds at the youngest ages.

SPECTATORS' OBSERVATIONS: DAVID WHALEY AND JAMES EDWARDS

At this point, the writer wants to stray from the discussions with the competitors and share some observations by a couple of the literally thousands of individuals who visited the pool daily for fun but were never members of the Sharks. Carl Frederick, Sr., and Moses Felder were two such individuals. The writer had the opportunity to meet both individuals over a year ago. Moses introduced the writer to Carl.

Moses Felder has operated Hill's Barber Shop on Elmwood Avenue for nearly sixty years and is a fixture in Columbia, and, in particular, the Black community. He is highly respected, and sitting in the barbershop, listening to Moses and his customers, is an experience this writer recommends to every individual. Both Moses and Carl shared and reinforced what the reader has previously heard or could imagine about the community that existed at Drew pool. Both men shared that they virtually spent their summers at Drew swimming and playing in the water. Both have so many positive memories that it appears as though it was yesterday that they were at the pool.

Moses shared that he made so many friends who remain today. He shared that he was invited to the Cape by Charles Bolden, Jr. to watch the launch of one of his flights. That's the closeness developed at Drew pool.

Each man shared stories about the lifeguards, confirming everything the reader has learned about the Drew pool staff. They reinforced the professionalism, care, compassion, and support that the lifeguards provided to the boys and girls who visited daily. Even today, after all these years, they continue to maintain relationships with the lifeguards. The two men attended the pool almost from its inception in 1950. The two men spoke of the individuals who were Sharks as though they were each teammates. That's how close friends they were. Each knew which lifeguard played football, track, or basketball, and which high school activities individuals were involved in, whether student council, the science club, or the school paper. They also followed their careers after high school, reporting whether they attended a Big 10 university, an Ivy League university, or remained closer to home at South Carolina State, USC, or another institution of higher learning.

Their personal friendships extended well beyond the lifeguards as they shared stories of their peers who swam daily. They were truly aware of the status of those less fortunate and of the struggles and sacrifices they made to go to the pool each day. Names and stories from individuals such as Whaley, Domino, MacIntosh, Bolden, Kimpson, and Brown flowed from them as they had such positive memories. The two men confirmed and reinforced everything that had been shared by the competitors who swam throughout this work. They recalled the names of Sharks the reader has heard about previously.

It was Foxy who rescued a young Delano Boulware, then around eight, and gave him the nickname Domino, which he has carried with him for nearly seventy years. Archive records of swim meets at Drew Park are full of stories regarding the winning exploits of James Evans, in every age category and in numerous events. In almost every one, James Evans came in first place. Beyond a shadow of a doubt, Foxy was one of the best all-around athletes to ever swim as a Shark. Standing on the edge of the high dive or occupying the lifeguard chair, his presence was unforgettable. He was an imposing figure, personable and cordial, well-known for his generosity and kindness, and never met a stranger. He was friendly, well known, and a guy everyone could look up to as an example. To many of the young swimmers, he was a role model one could only hope to emulate in life.

It was David Whaley's football injury on the first play of the season, which required the removal of his spleen, and set Thaddeus Bell on his journey to becoming a doctor. In reading the stories shared, these young men made a difference to the lives of their friends, peers, and fellow Sharks. Each was a competitor and, as you will learn, made an impression on their communities and on their peers throughout their lives. For many, their exploits far exceeded Drew pool, as they excelled on the football field or in academic or life's endeavors.

As readers are aware, David Whaley grew up in Saxon Homes, as did many of his peers. You will recall that he and Thaddeus worked for two summers at the Girl Scout camp in North Carolina as lifeguards, thanks to a connection from the Drew staff, when the Drew pool had reached its limit on lifeguards. David was the captain of the football team at C.A. Johnson High School. David graduated from Allen University and went on to earn a PhD at Clemson University, being one of the institution's first Black graduates. He later became the dean of students at Benedict College and later served as the vice president for student affairs. The reader will soon learn how Grant Lewis benefited from his relationship with David. For Carl and Moses, these facts were common knowledge.

The writer could potentially complete a separate work on other members of the Sharks. One thing that hinders writing about more individuals is the inability to locate family members of Sharks who have passed. Generally, it is reasonable to share information about deceased individuals, provided the information is positive in nature. Nothing, though, is a guarantee from legal action from a family member or the estate of an individual. It is just the fact that we live in a litigious society, and permission should be granted from the individual or a family member prior to sharing information about them. There are names and stories this writer would have liked to share about other Sharks, had he been able to obtain that permission. Sadly, those stories will have to wait for another day.

RUPERT A. BROWN, JR.

1935 – 2010

SHARED BY HIS DAUGHTERS,
RENEE BROWN AND ENID BROWN-DAWKINS

Born in 1935 in Jacksonville, Florida, Rupert Brown is, to date, one of the two oldest members of the Drew Park Shark family whom this writer has had the fortune to "meet" and share his story. Rupert's family moved to Columbia when he was three years old. It is truly an honor to be in the position to share Rupert's personal history as a means of preserving his legacy.

The reader first learned of Rupert in Moses Hopkins's personal history, when it was revealed that both Moses and Rupert, as young boys, attended Camp Atwater in Massachusetts. Moses was ten years old, and Rupert was nine. Atwater was the oldest camp for African Americans in the United States, and it was there that the two learned to swim. The reader will recall that the two boys were later in each other's weddings. Rupert's story, like that of Moses Hopkins, needs to be shared.

Born fifteen years prior to the construction of Drew pool, Rupert would have been able to swim in the brand-new pool. John Brown, not related to Rupert, the reader knows, was hired as one of the pool's first lifeguards. Rupert was seventeen when he began swimming as a Shark, as the team was formally established in 1952, making him and Moses two of the first members of the team. Having said that, many would think Rupert's age would prevent him from being a member of the team. In actuality, there was no age limit or being considered "too old," as the senior category began at age seventeen, and individuals often swam well into their thirties and beyond. It was one of the most distinctive features of Drew that individuals were not only encouraged to learn to swim but also to remain swimmers throughout their lives.

So, in all honesty, Rupert could just be beginning his swimming career and have many years ahead of him for swimming. Add to his age and maturity, Rupert swam the backstroke. He chose one of the more difficult strokes for competitions, a stroke, as the reader knows well, that was named "controlled drowning" by Lindy Jeffcoat. In addition to swimming the backstroke, Rupert became a prolific diver, and scattered throughout Columbia are photographs of Rupert magnificently standing on the edge of a diving board or performing various dives. His daughter, Renee, says the family has a photograph of her dad climbing the diving board ladder and smiling at the camera. It is not surprising to learn, as well, that Rupert became a lifeguard at Drew pool and gave swimming lessons.

Rupert's family built a home on Lorick Avenue when he was young. His parents owned and operated a full-service restaurant on Gervais Street called Rupert's Grill. Rupert has a brother and a sister. Rupert attended Booker T. Washington High School and, upon graduation, enrolled at North Carolina A&T University, where he studied for a time but later returned to Columbia and earned his economics degree from Allen University. Rupert became an educator and established a career teaching inmates at the South Carolina Department of Corrections, where he worked and from where he retired. He was married to Alice N. Brown, who was an educator. Rupert has two daughters, Renee T. and Enid Brown Dawkins. Rupert has three grandsons. Renee's husband, Ronald, shared that Rupert helped him perfect his swimming strokes. It appears that once you are a swim instructor, you're always a swim instructor!

YOLANDE KEARSE LEWIS

In the vein of outstanding swimmers who competed at the Drew Park pool, there is, without any doubt, Yolande Kearse Lewis. By the age of five, Yolande had learned to swim and was already competing in the Midget category. With a "love of the water," Yolande went on to compete and be victorious throughout her swimming career as a Drew Park Shark. She was truly an outstanding sprinter in the water, generally swimming "her stroke," the freestyle. She was also competent in the breaststroke and backstroke and was respected as a great swimmer. She was tall and slender, with a strong flutter often enabling her to touch the wall first. Yolande swam in every division, including the older division, in which she swam into her late twenties and early thirties.

With Yolande, "first" became a defining trait. Yolande was one of Drew's first female lifeguards. Though other girls had met all the requirements to serve as a lifeguard, none had the opportunity to do so until Yolande and one other female during her era. Like the male lifeguards who preceded her, Yolande passed all the requirements for becoming a water safety instructor and lifeguard. If this wasn't enough for her notoriety, Yolande became the first to marry another Shark. Her husband, Grant Lewis, a Shark and a lifeguard at Drew Park, and Yolande were married in 1978. The couple has two children, Jusef and Aisha.

Born in 1958, Yolande and her family lived on Laurel Street. Yolande's father worked in the postal system and was active in the Army National Guard. He played an essential role in Yolande's swimming career. It was her father who took her to the pool each day. Two years after beginning to learn to swim, the family moved to the outskirts of town. That did not hamper her father's enthusiasm for her to swim, as he drove her, her siblings, and other neighborhood children to the pool each day. Beyond chauffeuring the children, Yolande's father spent an inordinate amount of time with her in the pool, becoming more of a swim teacher, a role he assumed after her morning swim lessons in her primary years. Working the evening shift gave her father the opportunity and time to spend with them at the pool. Her dad influenced his children and others to learn how to swim. He was very cognizant of the fact that they needed to learn how to respect and handle themselves in a body of water, but also learn, enjoy, and experience the benefits of knowing how to swim. Yolande grew up in a household with five children. Three of them were deemed Drew Pool Sharks: an older sister, LaVerda, a younger brother, Kevin, and, of course, Yolande.

Yolande's mother was an elementary teacher. She taught first grade, and future generations of youth would remind the family how she influenced their education. She also played a pivotal role in Yolande's swimming career as an encourager, an avid supporter, and a loving hairdresser after swimming. The latter was a role that she was not necessarily fond of, but in support of Yolande's swimming, she did it anyway with love and care.

Yolande attended Columbia High School with the ambition of earning a swimming scholarship to Johnson C. Smith University. There was only one scholarship offered for female swimmers, and she had her sights set on earning it. Unfortunately for her, she did not receive that coveted scholarship. However, another young lady who shared the honor of being among the first female lifeguards at Drew pool was the scholarship recipient. She was an equally strong competitor and truly deserving of that coveted award to attend Johnson C. Smith.

Yolande attended South Carolina State University for one year before transferring to the University of South Carolina, where she majored in physical education and earned a Bachelor of Science degree. In addition to her teaching career, Yolande served as a coach for various sports. She has coached basketball, volleyball, track and field, and, of course, swimming. Grant made a career in the United States Air Force, and they have traveled and lived in several places, including Tokyo, Japan, and Minot, North Dakota. She taught and coached in Tokyo, Japan, and Minot, North Dakota. She ended her employment career as an assistant director in an after-school and summer program for middle schoolers and teens.

Returning lastly to her time as a Shark and working at the Drew Park pool, Yolande fondly recalls just how much the pool was a huge influence in her life. She vividly recalls the lessons learned from working as a cashier and learning to manage money, to working the basket room, and, ultimately, serving as a lifeguard. The time spent swimming and the life lessons learned from being a part of the Drew pool staff will always be engraved in her heart, along with her admiration, love, and sincere gratitude for the management team. Drew's management team proved instrumental in teaching her valuable life lessons, especially regarding the development of a strong work ethic, which she carries today.

As the reader has learned throughout these personal histories, the Drew Park pool influenced the swimmers in ways well beyond just learning to swim. The pool and staff, including the lifeguards, created an atmosphere of a loving and caring community and rewarded excellence in the pool with lasting memories and a legacy that endures.

GRANT LEWIS

Grant Lewis is sort of one of a kind when it comes to being a Shark. Grant was, in addition to being a Drew Pool Shark, a Greenview Dolphin for part of his swimming career.

Born in 1957, he lived with his mother and five siblings in Saxon Homes. Grant was introduced to the water by his Uncle James, better known to Drew Pool Sharks as Foxy, who threw him in the deep end and told him to kick his feet. That experience jump-started his swimming career. He knew he was either going to sink or swim; he obviously chose the latter.

He began going to Drew Park pool around the age of eight. Raising the twenty-five-cent daily entry fee always seemed challenging. However, there was always a staff member around who would pick up the slack, which allowed him entry into the pool. Once he gained entrance, he would go to the shallow end, hold on to the wall, and imitate the action of other swimmers. He boasts that he is a self-taught swimmer. His only instructors were the wall and ladder in 3 feet of water. However, had it not been for the kindness of the pool staff, he would not have been able to access the pool or use the wall and ladder as his teaching aids.

Around 1970, his family moved to the Greenview community, and there he would obtain his first job and experience as a Dolphin. David Whaley, a former Shark, gave him his first job experience. He would do odd jobs around the park, and it was David who paid him out of his own pocket. Grant eventually became a lifeguard, joined the Greenview Dolphins swim team, and became a Dolphin threat to the Drew Park Sharks.

Grant played football with his Drew Pool Shark friends, Stanley and Stephen McIntosh and Tim Harkness, who, in addition to playing football, were lifeguards. The group of friends was known for packing into Stanley's station wagon after football practice, and it was during one of those rides that the guys convinced Grant to return to Drew. Grant became a lifeguard and a Drew Park Shark, swimming distance races. He was a good swimmer, competing regularly with Ellis Pearson and Lindy Jeffcoat. Those two were renowned swimmers, with Ellis being a strong distance swimmer as outlined in his personal history. Grant said he recalled beating Ellis on one occasion, but as good as he was, his competition was often stronger.

Although Grant was the nephew of James "Foxy" Evans, one of the most beloved Sharks ever, he was not privy to the opportunity of having him as a real swim instructor, except for his first encounter with the water. By the time he started going to the pool, his Uncle James had joined the United States Navy and was out to sea on a nuclear submarine. Yolande recalls they always called him Uncle James and never Foxy, but to most people who swam at Drew and knew him, he was Foxy. There is hardly a personal history in this collection in which someone did not mention or credit Foxy for some aspect of his swimming and lifeguarding experiences. He was known to all and admired and respected by everyone. Grant felt fortunate to have him as his uncle.

Grant attended Keenan High School and, during his senior year, began dating Yolande Kearse. Clearly, the Drew Park pool played an integral part not only in his life but also in that of his future wife.

Grant loved football, and he was an outstanding player. He was a linebacker/defensive cornerback on the team. Following high school, Grant was awarded a scholarship as a walk-on at Virginia Union University, but soon realized that being on a college football team was more like a job than just having fun, and he realized this was not the life for him.

After a couple of years in the civilian workforce, on the sound advice of his Uncle James "Foxy," he decided to join the Air Force and make it his career. Joining the Air Force afforded him the opportunity to travel the country and see different parts of the world, being stationed in places like Florida, Colorado, Alaska, Korea, Japan, and his home state, South Carolina. He also served in Desert Shield/Desert Storm. His final tour of duty was at Minot AFB, where he retired and transitioned from active duty to civilian life in Huntsville, Alabama. There, he used his military experience and skills and retired as a network engineer from SAIC. Grant has many fond memories of Drew pool, his coworkers, and the individuals whose lives he had the opportunity to touch by sharing his swimming skills. However, the one thing he is most grateful for is meeting the love of his life at Drew pool, and they have shared almost forty-eight years of marriage.

LAVERDA KEARSE JAMES

As the reader learned from Yolande, her sister, LaVerda, swam as a Shark at Drew pool. LaVerda said she loved the water as much as her sister but wasn't as competitive. She fondly recalled her swim lessons each day. Like her sister, though, LaVerda focused on her dad's contribution to her swimming. There was no doubt about her father's passion for ensuring the family could swim. Her father had learned to swim in the Army and developed in his children endurance and "no fear of deep water." It was her dad's belief that no child of his would ever drown for lack of knowing how to swim. LaVerda recalls the family's move from Laurel Street to Riverview Terrace near the Broad River, where he continued to drive them to Drew pool daily.

When one worked at Drew Park, they had to be willing to do every job. The staff at Drew Park pool was always small, well-trained, and obedient. It was demanded of them. LaVerda indicated she worked in the basket room and did whatever was required of her. She wasn't sure if she passed the lifeguard certification requirements. She was told she did not; there was a certificate, but it was never signed by the chief guard and never given to her. She would never have been allowed to sit in the lifeguard chair at that time, whether she passed or not, except possibly to relieve a male guard who went on a lunch or bathroom break. (Complete gender bias was in full effect in the late 60s.) However, she was given the opportunity to teach swimming lessons. At all meets, LaVerda served as the statistician, recording event times and the order of finishers. She worked in the office, on occasion, so assuming that role was just the expectation. She was a very thorough individual, so her skills were appreciated in taking on that responsibility. In addition, she never complained about the opportunity to "watch the boys" compete.

As you will recall, LaVerda was Yolande's older sister by five years, having been born in 1953. LaVerda's preferred stroke was the backstroke. This writer had to chuckle since he recalled Lindy Jeffcoat referring to the backstroke as "controlled drowning." LaVerda said she also liked swimming the breaststroke. She swam in most age categories until high school graduation, and she worked her final summer at Drew pool her senior year. LaVerda mentioned that her nephew, and son of Yolande, Jusef Lewis, is often referred to in the family as the "Butterfly King." She mentioned that, in reference to her memory of both Lindy Jeffcoat and "Ray" Ellis Pearson, they were the masters of her time. Her memory was vivid as she recalled how strong of swimmers those two young men were. In particular, she noted that Ray had overtaken Jimmie Ruff for the title with his outstanding skills in the water.

LaVerda attended St. Martin Catholic School for elementary from the second to eighth grade. She was an exceptional student for many reasons, not the least of which was the time her mother, a teacher, spent with her. She entered elementary school at the age of five; thus, she was younger than many of her counterparts at the pool.

She attended Dreher High School. Dreher was on the way to her mother's job as a first-grade teacher. Dreher was renowned for its location within the community. It had an outstanding reputation; thus, it made sense to the family for her to attend that school. The high school was also known to many college recruiters who visited to interview potential students.

Mrs. Ethel Bolden was the school librarian, and she made it her duty to notify Black students who might not have been informed about potential recruiters visiting on any given day. Dreher was one of the schools under mandatory desegregation. One day, while recruiters from the University of Pennsylvania were visiting the school, Mrs. Bolden literally grabbed LaVerda and handed her Penn's information. She interviewed with the University of Pennsylvania staff and was offered the most scholarship funds of any university. Upon graduation, she went to Philadelphia.

At the university, LaVerda majored in urban studies (city planning) with a minor in social psychology. LaVerda did not swim in college, nor could she remember if the campus even had a pool. She had intentions to attend law school but returned to Columbia and married someone from high school. He was not a swimmer. She continued to be a recreational swimmer in the summers after high school and during college.

LaVerda's first job following college graduation was with a financial services organization, and she worked with both federal and state social service agencies, including HHS and the Social Security Administration. She interviewed with the FBI but declined the offer after learning she would be working in Detroit. LaVerda moved to Charleston and is currently employed as a supervising paralegal at the Center for Heirs Property, a nonprofit. It's an amazing organization focused on educating people about the importance of land, helping protect land and clear titles, providing legal services for family land, and serving as a resource and advisor on estate planning and wills. The work ensures that families can maintain control of family property and that it is not taken from them. This has become a major issue for farmers and families: maintaining legal ownership of their family's property.

LaVerda has two sons and a stepdaughter. Her sons swim, and the older son was the chief guard for the North Charleston pool. Her son, who was the chief guard, has asthma, and swimming has essential benefits for maintaining healthy lung capacity for people with chronic lung and respiratory issues. This writer will add this information to the earlier comments about the benefits of swimming to the general population. The writer would note as well that this son's name is in the Drew records, as he swam with the Sharks one summer, upon his grandfather's insistence. LaVerda's younger son is an excellent swimmer, but he said he was going break the family curse of having to work at the pool and do something different.

However, enough of reading this writer's summary of the conversation with Laverda Kearse James. For the final two conversations of this work, let's take the opportunity to hear directly from the contributors as each has chosen to share his or her personal journey as a Drew Park Shark. After all, who better to help the reader understand the intricacies of life at the pool?

"What I Know by LaVerda Kearse James

When my sister contacted me about this project, she began by saying that some guy was interviewing former members of the Drew Pool Sharks about their experiences and their memories of the park and the pool. I wondered how I could possibly share anything that would compare to the glorious stories of victory my peers and family members would share. I was only a proficient swimmer, meaning I was good enough to compete but not good enough to break any records or make the newspaper. I was good enough to teach, but not good enough to even consider a swimming scholarship. I was good enough to help coach, but I would never have my picture on the wall of fame or be remembered by more than just a handful of people. If Yolande Lewis were not my sister, I am fairly certain that I would not have had this opportunity, nor would I have taken the time to stroll back down memory lane and really think about what those six or seven summers of my life meant to me, and how those pool experiences helped shape my life.

I remember vividly that my father took the then four of us to the park a few times when I was very young and my sister was barely a toddler as a summer treat and to escape the sometimes-brutal heat of Columbia, South Carolina. (There would eventually be seven of us, five children and my parents, and yes, every child had to learn to swim.) The park and the pool were within easy walking distance of the small upstairs apartment we lived in on Laurel Street. My mother would sometimes stand in the sprinkler with my baby sister, but I was drawn to the fence surrounding the pool. I loved and dreamed of being in what appeared to be the clear blue, cool waters. My father eventually took us to the pool. I remember my father riding my sister on his shoulders and "swishing" me around by my arms from side to side. I'm sure that it was on one of those rare occasions that the pool manager talked to my parents about letting us take swimming lessons, and as Shakespeare's Julius Caesar said, "The die was cast."

My father learned to swim in the United States Army, but he was determined that his children and wife would learn to be more than basic swimmers. (Let it be noted that his wife, our mother, though supportive, was having none of that face-in-water stuff.) Nevertheless, my sister and I began taking lessons around 1962 or 1963, and until I graduated from high school in 1970, every summer was spent at the Drew pool, taking lessons, competing in pool swim meets, and eventually working there. I remember that my first teachers were the pool manager, and then lifeguard Jimmie Ruff, and my father, sometimes in the water, and sometimes at the fence yelling instructions. The downside was that my mother had to comb through the tangled mess our hair became after a morning in the water. (My poor mother, all but one of us had a "mess" of hair.)

By the time I became a decent swimmer, my younger sister had become a super swimmer in the Midget Girls category. I knew by the time I began swimming in the Senior Women category that I was not super competitive in the water, and that I enjoyed watching the competition among the other swimmers and divers more than I loved practicing and swimming laps for hours simply to compete in a 55-yard race. Those hours of training did teach me perseverance, just as I was promised it would, and it did build endurance, just as I was told it would, but it did not make me love the competition. I did win some races, primarily in the breaststroke and backstroke categories, but loved cheering for my sister and other younger children I worked with more, and I absolutely loved watching the older "men" (boys) fight for dominance in the water. I enjoyed sitting on the sidelines, under the tent, keeping statistics during swim meets, and organizing the meet records and swimmers' records for the office. I did not know that any of that "scut" work would someday have a historical context. Nor could I have known that keeping those records would foreshadow my lifelong career organizing and designing administrative systems, handling finances, researching legal issues, etc.—"scut" work on a different level.

It never occurred to me as a child or teenager that Drew swimmers were an anomaly. Of course, I recognized that we were segregated from other swimmers. We knew that there was another city pool across town that we were not allowed to visit, and that we would never have the opportunity to test our skills or speed against their team. But our lives had always been segregated, so the unnatural felt normal. We were continuously praised and encouraged as swimmers. It was always affirmed to us that, if given the chance, we would more than likely win against the Maxcy-Gregg swimmers and that there was no distance swimmer at Maxcy-Gregg or anywhere, Black, White, or otherwise, who could beat Jimmie Ruff in a long-distance race. Whether true or not, we absolutely believed that! Our coaches had faith in us as swimmers.

This belief was also evident throughout the staff, and that created the "trickle down" economics of self-confidence, self-worth, and pride that the majority culture we lived in tried to deny us. It never occurred to me to question why there were no female lifeguards; when girls passed the lifeguard training courses, they still never sat in a chair. However, we were living in a time and in a culture where men, black or white, were elevated, and women's roles were just beginning to change. It was always made clear that anyone hired to work at the pool would have to be willing to do whatever they were asked, but it was also clear that the lifeguards were at the top of the food chain. I never made it to the top of the chain, but I developed a work ethic that is simple, even if the task is unpleasant. If you know up front what is expected before you take the job, then do the job you are paid to do. That is not to imply that anyone should take any job, but I learned early that no job is perfect and all work can be meaningful.

Regardless of the limitations imposed on the Sharks by the times and the culture, what the swim program accomplished was nothing short of remarkable. Why would parents drop off, walk, or send their children to a public park or pool before the Carolina sun was high in the sky and leave them in the hands of sixteen- to twenty-three-year-olds until the sun began to disappear below the horizon? How is it that the children of doctors, teachers, housekeepers, sanitation workers, and under-employed families could all come together to form what would become the springboard to success for those children? How did an underfunded, unrecognized, and understaffed summer program give rise to adults who not only had, or could have had, meaningful careers but who also retained a sense of community?

I don't know that I have the answers, but here is what I do know. My life was shaped by men like my father, who made the sacrifice to drive not only his children but also any child who asked for a ride to Drew pool because he believed that our children should have the opportunity to learn a sport previously reserved for the "other side" of town. And he fiercely believed that our children, his especially, were equal to any child. Like our coaches, who seemed to know without a shadow of a doubt that swimming would provide a way out of limited circumstances for children. It just required that they be trained and nurtured by people who truly cared not only about their prowess in the water but also about their character development and their general well-being. Young men like Jimmie Ruff and Talmadge Dixon tried to train younger swimmers and divers with the same techniques their teachers used to motivate their gifted students to achieve excellence. Whether those students had equal abilities or not, they still received equal training and sometimes equal criticism. Though it may have been harsh, swimmers always felt safe in the space known as Drew pool under their tutelage. Women like my mother and others who, while not at the pool every day, were there for almost every competition. They came with their umbrellas for shade, sun hats for protection, coolers filled with sandwiches, snacks, and sodas, and a thermos of water, which they brought not for their children but for all children who might want or need it. They understood that not every child's parent could or would be there to support. So, they were there, sitting, feeding, sweating, and cheering loudly for *all* the Sharks.

Watching swimmers like Jimmie Ruff glide through the water, or the younger Ben Jeffcoat propel his upper body like some giant butterfly, or seeing my younger sister freestyle using her incredible fast flutter kick past girls much older and win in the 55-yard freestyle, or watching the beautiful aerial gymnastics of divers like Talmadge

Dixon—these are memories that this project brought to the surface of my very long memory. The pride in knowing that my sister broke the gender barrier by becoming the first recognized female lifeguard with her Water Safety Instructors' certification in hand, the wonder of watching my brother compete successfully with other young people of all genders and races all over the state, the satisfaction of seeing both of my sons complete the mile-plus swim required to attain the status of Eagle Scout (my older son went on to become one of North Charleston's Chief Lifeguards), the wonder of watching Stanley McIntosh race up and down the deck encouraging his swimmers to "kick, pull" (one coach was famous for yelling at kids, "Don't run on the deck" and "Kick, pull, glide"), and the amazement that even at the age of sixty-nine or older, former stars like "Ray" Ellis Pearson were still swimming miles a day and still interested in the well-being of a new generation of swimmers. These are the things that define the legacy of Drew pool and the Sharks for me. What I know now, but did not know way back then, was the sacrifice, the energy, the drive, the dedication, and the courage that early staff, as well as every parent or guardian who entrusted their children to Drew pool, were attributes that touched the lives of every Drew Pool Shark I know. It broke my heart to see the original pool filled in and re-purposed, but it gladdens my heart to know that the spirit and the pride of the Drew Sharks continue.

This is what I know."

JUSEF "JD" LEWIS

Readers have certainly learned by now how competitive swimming has benefited men and women (boys and girls) since the opening of Drew Park pool. From becoming a Shark to learning valuable life lessons through his employment as a lifeguard and as an outstanding sprinter in the pool, JD was recruited by the Columbia Fire Department Swift Water Rescue team before being selected as a special agent in the United States Secret Service Rescue Swimmer program. JD was the only Black member of the city's Swift Water Rescue team.

Jusef, or JD as he is called, was born in Columbia in 1978. He is the son of Grant and Yolande Lewis. JD says he probably learned to walk and swim around the same time. Undoubtedly, his Shark father was a force in his life and influenced his swimming. Having watched JD take to the water and learn to swim, JD says his daddy threw him into the deep end of the pool. JD was afraid of the deep water, but his father had confidence in his ability and proved his daddy correct as he swam to the side of the pool. JD proudly declares he is fully aware he grew up in an "irregular family" of Black swimmers. He swam some at the Greenview pool but spent most of his time at the Drew Park pool. He emphatically states, "It was a grand opportunity" and "fun in the sun." It wasn't long before JD was competing as a Shark. He was one of the faster swimmers on the team. JD was a very talented swimmer, and after turning fifteen, he often chose to swim against older kids to improve his skills. He was a sprinter preferring the butterfly and freestyle, thus swam the shorter distances or sprint races.

JD is the first Shark to share that he swam in the "new" outdoor Drew pool following the demolition of the original pool due to age-related issues. He shares that he swam in the original pool and its replacement. Like the original, it was a 50-meter pool. One difference with the new pool was its shape. It was an L-shaped pool with the long arm being 50 meters and deeper, while the shorter arm of the pool was shallow. The pool was built in a different direction from the original pool. It appeared to be rotated sideways compared to the original pool. With JD's swimming prowess, it should be no surprise that he served as a lifeguard and was WSI certified. This was during the early to mid-nineties, but nothing had changed in terms of what was expected of lifeguards. The guards did it all, whatever was needed. He would clean the bathroom toilets or the pool, work the basket room if needed, and sit in the chair.

Like so many before him, JD said the Drew Park pool taught him so many life lessons and shaped his development. He credits his experience at Drew for instilling responsibility, character, discipline, and a work ethic, traits that directly impacted his professional life as both a fireman and a Secret Service agent. At the pool, he cleaned with a weight belt and a vacuum. He said he felt like a chemist or a hazmat employee as he "shocked" the water with pH tablets, which he broke and added to the water. There were also 55-gallon drums of chlorine. This was generally necessary around midday after the pool's exposure to the sun and people. As the reader is fully aware, the pool was always packed with guests. JD said you would meet people from all walks of life at Drew. He credits his interactions with professionals, such as teachers, doctors, lawyers, and judges at Drew, for offering him everything he could aspire to be. It was these professions and professionals that he saw potentially in himself. It was truly motivating for

JD to see so many people who looked like him, a young Black boy growing up in the South. It was truly where "everyone came together," and to JD, it was "home."

JD worked each summer through high school. He continued to swim competitively as it was his "first" sport. After a loss to one young man in a race, he talked to his coach and "godfather," Stanley McIntosh, who told him that the other swimmer was not better than him. The other swimmer had one advantage, though, as he, unlike JD, swam in an indoor pool all year long, while JD could only swim the summer months at Drew pool. Having learned this, JD decided to swim at Harbison Aquatics on the other side of town. He and his sister, Aisha, were just about the only two Black members at Harbison. Swimming at Harbison allowed JD to develop skill and strength beyond his previous conditioning, and when he again swam competitively at Drew, few could match his skill, speed, and strength. He was later promoted to head lifeguard at the Drew pool.

An interesting note about Harbison Aquatics was that there were award-winning swimmers among its ranks. One such individual was Heath Edwards. Heath later became the coach of the University of South Carolina Gamecocks, being named Coach of the Year in 2017 and 2018. He began swimming in high school, and for his age group, he had a very successful career. He won the 200-meter butterfly at Junior Nationals as a sophomore at Irmo High School, and in his junior year, he finished in the top two in the country in two other events.

Again, the reader is aware that JD's father, Grant, was in the Air Force and stationed in Japan for a couple of years. JD served as a lifeguard on the base's pool for his first two years of high school. He graduated from Keenan High School in Columbia and attended Livingstone College in Salisbury, North Carolina, on a football and track scholarship for his first two years. He transferred to Benedict College for his remaining two years and worked as a lifeguard at Drew and Benedict College pools. It was following graduation that JD was recruited to join the Columbia Fire Department's Swift Water Rescue team. He was a fireman first and foremost, and he served with the department from 2003 to 2010. During that time, JD became a Haz Mat Tech and a Swift Water Rescue Tech and was certified to ride the Rescue 1 truck. He moved to working as a deputy sheriff for Richland County and continued to work part-time as a lifeguard for the next six years before applying to be a United States Secret Service Special Agent. He entered a six-week Coast Guard training program and became the fourth-ever Black Elite Rescue Swimmer in history. JD has been employed by the Secret Service since 2015. This is all the product of a young man who began his swimming career at the Drew Park pool.

From the outset of this unique story and, in particular, this unique individual, this writer has attempted to demonstrate the journey and the memorable impact the Drew Park pool experience had on JD. To date, only his aunt LaVerda has offered to share her personal and emotional prose to highlight that journey. That is, until now. This writer wants the reader to truly hear—in his words—thus JD shares these words:

> "Remembering back on my childhood, it seems as if I was walking and swimming simultaneously. As far back as I can recollect, aquatics has been a part of my life. Some notable memories were of my father, also a swimmer, teaching me at a young age to trust in my abilities. He would thrust me into the deep end of the pool, a symbolic and very literal "sink or swim" evolution. Encouraging me to conquer the fear of things that were hard or frightening to me, I could already swim, but I was only comfortable in the shallow end of the pool,

where I could always put my feet down, and it was safe. It wasn't until maturing later in life that I understood the duality of the lesson taught then. It was also later that I came to understand how seemingly rare it was for an African American to be versed in swimming. I come from a lineage of swimmers. Both my parents swam competitively, as did several other family members. As swimming goes, it was my first sport, and all I knew to that point were Black swimmers. To me, Black people and swimming were the norm, and at the heart of it all was Drew Park Pool.

It was in my formative years at Drew pool that I was introduced to the core values of hard work, responsibility, discipline, competition, the thrill of victory, and the agony of defeat. Unfortunately, it was also here that I tasted the deep-seated bitterness of racism. Unbeknownst to me at the time, the life lessons and values would help shape my future self.

Drew pool was a myriad of African Americans from all walks of life. There was no truer representation of the vast possibilities of what we were, what we could aspire to be, and what we could fall victim to becoming. From the ladies of the night, street pharmacists, local thugs, to prominent lawyers, doctors, school board members, coaches, teachers, etc., Drew pool was a place, and a moment in time, where no matter your occupation or social status, there was a commonality and a camaraderie that superseded the outside world. It was a positive image and an influence that was needed, especially for a young Black boy coming up in the deep south.

Life guarding was my first job, and as of writing this, it is my longest-standing job, with twenty-one years of experience, working in that capacity from the age of fifteen to thirty-six. With the help of so many people, specifically my coaches, swimming and lifeguarding have given me opportunities I wouldn't have otherwise had. As I mentioned previously, the rarity of a Black swimmer has made being a swimmer somewhat of a commodity. I entered a career with the City of Columbia Fire Department under the premise that I would train to become a swift water rescue technician, as there weren't any Black people in the division at that time. I eventually became a swift water rescue technician and an asset to that division.

Over time, I evolved into a career in federal law enforcement. I was again encouraged to attend a selection for a rescue swimmer position. The rescue swim school is notoriously known to be extremely difficult. It's a very small elite group of special agents inside the agency who have become rescue swimmers. Through the lessons of hard work and mental fortitude developed after years at Drew pool, I became the fourth African American rescue swimmer with the Secret Service. Serving in this elite unit has afforded me the opportunity to serve in different capacities close to several U.S. presidents. Drew pool, the multitude of positive influences there, and the support I received have directly affected my career opportunities, and I am forever grateful."

CONCLUSION

The city of Columbia should be commended for building Drew Park and providing African American citizens with such a magnificent swimming pool and park amenities. Clearly, the city's approach to being proactive during this tumultuous period in history went a long way toward preventing the racial strife seen in cities throughout the South, such as Birmingham, Greensboro, Selma, and Nashville. Over the decades, the only thing the Sharks ever really wanted was an opportunity. With leadership and guidance, with love, affection, and support, the Sharks provided the teamwork, discipline, perseverance, commitment, determination, and resolve to be a great team, to possess a winning attitude, and to have a winning outlook on life. These stories are proof that, given opportunity, success can be the outcome of overcoming whatever challenges are placed before you. This writer has been truly inspired by the stories he had the honor to hear. It is his hope that future generations read about the individuals who maximized their capabilities with that opportunity. A special thanks to Stanley McIntosh for his encouragement, his wish to have the Sharks' stories told, and for his friendship and support through this amazing journey. Thanks as well to Lindy, Gary, and Ellis for the encouragement and support throughout this entire project. A huge thanks goes to each and every former Shark who was willing to give of their time for an outstanding and informative conversation. Thanks as well to Freddie and Regina Brandyburg for their assistance with the editing and their constant support.

APPENDIX

JIM CROW LAWS:

At the start of the 1880s, big cities in the South were not wholly beholden to Jim Crow laws, and Black Americans found more freedom in them.

This led to substantial Black populations moving to the cities and, as the decade progressed, white city dwellers demanded more laws to limit opportunities for African Americans.

Jim Crow laws soon spread around the country with even more force than previously. Public parks were forbidden for African Americans to enter, and theaters and restaurants were segregated.

Segregated waiting rooms in bus and train stations were required, as well as water fountains, restrooms, building entrances, elevators, cemeteries, and even amusement-park cashier windows.

Laws forbade African Americans from living in white neighborhoods. Segregation was enforced for public pools, phone booths, hospitals, asylums, jails, and residential homes for the elderly and handicapped.

Some states required separate textbooks for Black and white students. New Orleans mandated the segregation of prostitutes according to race. In Atlanta, African Americans in court were given a different Bible from white people to swear on. Marriage and cohabitation between white and Black people were strictly forbidden in most Southern states.

From the 1880s into the 1960s, most American states enforced segregation through Jim Crow laws, so called after a black character in minstrel shows. From Delaware to California, and from North Dakota to Texas, many states (and cities, too) could impose legal punishments on people for consorting with members of another race. The most common types of laws forbade intermarriage and ordered business owners and public institutions to keep their black and white clientele separated. Here is a sampling of laws from various states.

Nurses: No person or corporation shall require any white female nurse to nurse in wards or rooms in hospitals, either public or private, in which negro men are placed. Alabama

Buses: All passenger stations in this state operated by any motor transportation company shall have separate waiting rooms or spaces and separate ticket windows for the white and colored races. Alabama

Railroads: The conductor of each passenger train is authorized and required to assign each passenger to the car or the division of the car, when it is divided by a partition, designated for the race to which such passenger belongs. Alabama

Restaurants: It shall be unlawful to conduct a restaurant or other place for the serving of food in the city, at which white and colored people are served in the same room, unless such white and colored persons are effectually separated by a solid partition extending from the floor upward to a distance of seven feet or higher, and unless a separate entrance from the street is provided for each compartment. Alabama

Pool and Billiard Rooms: It shall be unlawful for a negro and a white person to play together or in company with each other at any game of pool or billiards. Alabama

Toilet Facilities, Male: Every employer of white or negro males shall provide for such white or negro males reasonably accessible and separate toilet facilities.

Juvenile Delinquents: There shall be separate buildings, not nearer than one-fourth mile to each other, one for white boys and one for negro boys. White boys and negro boys shall not, in any manner, be associated together or worked together. Florida

Mental Hospitals: The Board of Control shall see that proper and distinct apartments are arranged for said patients, so that in no case shall Negroes and white persons be together. Georgia

Intermarriage: It shall be unlawful for a white person to marry anyone except a white person. Any marriage in violation of this section shall be void. Georgia

Barbers: No colored barber shall serve as a barber to white women or girls. Georgia

Burial: The officer in charge shall not bury, or allow to be buried, any colored persons upon ground set apart or used for the burial of white persons. Georgia

Restaurants: All persons licensed to conduct a restaurant shall serve either white people exclusively or colored people exclusively and shall not sell to the two races within the same room or serve the two races anywhere under the same license. Georgia

Amateur Baseball: It shall be unlawful for any amateur white baseball team to play baseball on any vacant lot or baseball diamond within two blocks of a playground devoted to the Negro race, and it shall be unlawful for any amateur-colored baseball team to play baseball in any vacant lot or baseball diamond within two blocks of any playground devoted to the white race. Georgia

Parks: It shall be unlawful for colored people to frequent any park owned or maintained by the city for the benefit, use, and enjoyment of white persons…and unlawful for any white person to frequent any park owned or maintained by the city for the use and benefit of colored persons. Georgia

Wine and Beer: All persons licensed to conduct the business of selling beer or wine…shall serve either white people exclusively or colored people exclusively and shall not sell to the two races within the same room at any time. Georgia

Circus Tickets: All circuses, shows, and tent exhibitions, to which the attendance of…more than one race is invited or expected to attend shall provide for the convenience of its patrons not less than two ticket offices with individual ticket sellers, and not less than two entrances to the said performance, with individual ticket takers and receivers, and in the case of outside or tent performances, the said ticket offices shall not be less than twenty-five (25) feet apart. Louisiana

Housing: Any person…who shall rent any part of any such building to a negro person or a negro family when such building is already in whole or in part in occupancy by a white person or white family, or vice versa when the building is in occupancy by a negro person or negro family, shall be guilty of a misdemeanor and on conviction thereof shall be punished by a fine of not less than twenty-five ($25.00) nor more than one hundred ($100.00) dollars or be imprisoned not less than 10, or more than 60 days, or both such fine and imprisonment in the discretion of the court. Louisiana

The Blind: The board of trustees shall...maintain a separate building...on separate ground for the admission, care, instruction, and support of all blind persons of the colored or black race. Louisiana

Education: Separate schools shall be maintained for the children of the white and colored races. Mississippi

Promotion of Equality: Any person...who shall be guilty of printing, publishing or circulating printed, typewritten or written matter urging or presenting for public acceptance or general information, arguments or suggestions in favor of social equality or of intermarriage between whites and negroes, shall be guilty of a misdemeanor and subject to fine or not exceeding five hundred (500.00) dollars or imprisonment not exceeding six (6) months or both. Mississippi

Intermarriage: The marriage of a white person with a negro or mulatto or person who shall have one-eighth or more of negro blood shall be unlawful and void. Mississippi

Hospital Entrances: There shall be maintained by the governing authorities of every hospital maintained by the state for treatment of white and colored patients separate entrances for white and colored patients and visitors, and such entrances shall be used by the race only for which they are prepared. Mississippi

Prisons: The warden shall see that the white convicts shall have separate apartments for both eating and sleeping from the negro convicts. Mississippi

Textbooks: Books shall not be interchangeable between the white and colored schools but shall continue to be used by the race first using them. North Carolina

Libraries: The state librarian is directed to fit up and maintain a separate place for the use of the colored people who may come to the library for the purpose of reading books or periodicals. North Carolina

Militia: The white and colored militia shall be separately enrolled and shall never be compelled to serve in the same organization. No organization of colored troops shall be permitted where white troops are available, and while white permitted to be organized, colored troops shall be under the command of white officers. North Carolina

Transportation: The…Utilities Commission…is empowered and directed to require the establishment of separate waiting rooms at all stations for the white and colored races. North Carolina

Lunch Counters: No persons, firms, or corporations who or which furnish meals to passengers at station restaurants or station eating houses, in times limited by common carriers of said passengers, shall furnish said meals to white and colored passengers in the same room, or at the same table, or at the same counter. South Carolina

Child Custody: It shall be unlawful for any parent, relative, or other white person in this State, having the control or custody of any white child, by right of guardianship, natural or acquired, or otherwise, to dispose of, give, or surrender such white child permanently into the custody, control, maintenance, or support, of a negro. South Carolina

Theaters: Every person…operating…any public hall, theatre, opera house, motion picture show or any place of public entertainment or public assemblage which is attended by both white and colored persons, shall separate the white race and the colored race and shall set apart and designate…certain seats therein to be occupied by white persons and a portion thereof, or certain seats therein, to be occupied by colored persons. Virginia